GLUTEN FREE

GOOD HOUSEKEEPING

GLUTEN FREE

EASY & DELICIOUS RECIPES FOR EVERY MEAL

★ GOOD FOOD GUARANTEED ★

HEARST BOOKS
New York

HEARST BOOKS
New York

An Imprint of Sterling Publishing
1166 Avenue of the Americas
New York, NY 10036

Good Housekeeping is a registered trademark of Hearst Communications, Inc.

ISBN : 978-1-61837-199-7

GOOD HOUSEKEEPING

Jane Francisco
EDITOR IN CHIEF
Melissa Geurts
DESIGN DIRECTOR
Susan Westmoreland
FOOD DIRECTOR

Cover Design: Chris Thompson and Jen Cogliantry
Series Design: Yeon Kim
Layout Design: Gretchen Achilles
Project Editor: Andrea Lynn

The Good Housekeeping Cookbook Seal guarantees that the recipes in this cookbook meet the strict standards of the Good Housekeeping Research Institute. The Institute has been a source of reliable information and a consumer advocate since 1900, and established its seal of approval in 1909. Every recipe has been triple-tested for ease, reliability, and great taste.

For information about custom editions, special sales, premium and corporate purchases, please contact Sterling Special Sales Department at 800-805-5489 or specialsales@sterlingpublishing.com.

Distributed in Canada by Sterling Publishing
c/o Canadian Manda Group, 165 Dufferin Street
Toronto, Ontario, Canada M6K 3H6
Distributed in Australia by Capricorn Link (Australia) Pty. Ltd.
P.O. Box 704, Windsor, NSW 2756 Australia

Manufactured in China

www.sterlingpublishing.com

CONTENTS

FOREWORD 7

INTRODUCTION 8

Breakfasts & Brunches 13

Hearty Sandwiches & Salads 27

Soups & Stews 43

Stovetop Suppers 57

Grilled Favorites 77

Bakes & Casseroles 95

Sweet & Fruity Finales 113

INDEX 124

PHOTOGRAPHY CREDITS 126

METRIC CONVERSION CHARTS 127

Tangerine Beef Stir-Fry
(page 65)

Foreword

Interest in a gluten-free lifestyle and products is at an all-time high. More people are being diagnosed with celiac disease, while others have discovered that they or a family member is experiencing sensitivity to gluten. And, yes, there has been a fad of gluten-free dieting as a weight-loss tool. All of those concerned are looking for advice on navigating their way through the grocery store and cooking their favorite foods with gluten-free ingredients.

My own interest in gluten-free products came about when a friend was diagnosed with celiac disease about a decade ago. I researched brands and trolled the supermarket reading labels, finding gluten in everything from chicken broth to candy bars. Suddenly I was on a mission to make delicious gluten-free food, from sauces to stuffing to desserts.

While Good Housekeeping doesn't endorse a gluten-free diet for the general population, we want to provide recipes and advice for those who need to be on one. So, we created *Gluten Free* to deliver tasty, healthful, gluten-free recipes for breakfasts, lunches, and dinners. Our introduction explores the low-down on gluten, along with tips on label reading and an exploration of gluten-free grains.

Then it's on to the recipes, including gluten-free takes on all of your favorites—pasta, stir-fries, barbecue, casseroles, burgers, and even pizza. Because baking gluten-free is a challenge, we provide a recipe for a simple all-purpose flour blend used in our banana bread, muffins, classic cookies, and more. Icons at the end of each recipe identify dishes you can make ahead 🍲 or prepare in 30 minutes or less 🕐. Low-cal ☺, heart-healthy ♥, and high-fiber recipes 🌿 are indicated, too. Whether you are eating gluten-free or cooking for someone who is, *Gluten Free* aims to take the worry out of gluten-free shopping and eating. So, check our ingredient lists, shop, and start cooking.

SUSAN WESTMORELAND
Food Director, *Good Housekeeping*

Introduction

WHAT IS GLUTEN?

A lot of people associate gluten with wheat, but that's only the beginning. Gluten is a protein found in wheat, rye, and barley. The particular sequence of amino acids that forms the protein can damage the gastrointestinal tracts of some people, even when eaten in small amounts. To avoid this protein and the damage it can wreak, people diagnosed with celiac disease (and others who are sensitive to gluten) must forgo eating gluten-containing foods. The restrictions include many staples—some of which would otherwise be important parts of a healthy diet, such as whole-grain products like breads and pastas. Standard cookies and baked goods are generally off-limits as well, along with products that may contain hidden amounts of gluten, such as candy, French fries, soy sauce, and many other store-bought condiments.

WHO BENEFITS FROM A GLUTEN-FREE DIET?

The recipes in this book make it straightforward to follow a gluten-free diet, providing meals that are satisfying, tasty, and absent of gluten proteins. People with celiac disease who need to follow a gluten-free diet to the letter will benefit from these recipes immediately. But for those with gluten sensitivities or wheat allergies, a total commitment to a gluten-free diet may not be necessary, and may even have some drawbacks. Different conditions warrant varying levels of concern about gluten in the diet, and following the recipes in this book can help you avoid gluten to the extent that is right for you. Before embarking on a gluten-free diet, you should see your doctor.

MAXIMIZING NUTRITION

Nutrient shortfalls due to poor absorption can be a major issue with celiac disease, and people on a gluten-free diet may need to take special steps to get enough of certain nutrients, especially those normally supplied by fortified grains. Work with your doctor and dietitian to make sure you're getting enough iron, thiamin, riboflavin, niacin, and folate, and ask for recommendations on supplements if you're falling short. It's important to get your doctor's advice on the right amounts for you, because your ability to absorb nutrients may be different from someone else's. If you have low bone density (a common issue with celiac disease), your doctor may also recommend a supplement of vitamin D, which helps to build calcium and strong bones. Have your team ascertain your fiber status as well: Because grains are restricted, people on a gluten-free diet often need to consume more fiber-rich foods. We make it easier: The recipes in this book feature a special icon that indicates high fiber content—those recipes containing 5 grams or more of fiber per serving.

BUYING GLUTEN-FREE

Gluten-free labeling has gotten a much-needed update in recent years. The Food and Drug Administration implemented a gluten-free label rule that requires foods marketing a gluten-free status to contain less than 20 parts per million (ppm) of gluten, currently the smallest amount that can reliably be detected. Allowed terms include "gluten-free," "without gluten," "no gluten," and "free of gluten." The definition provides consumers—especially those with celiac disease—the assurance that "gluten-free" claims

Spring
Vegetable
Risotto
with Shrimp
(page 70)

on food products will be consistent and reliable across the food industry.

To help make cooking easier for you, we provide gluten-free product suggestions within many of our recipes, though you may want to do some taste-testing to find the brands with the flavor and texture you like best. Cooking—and especially baking—from scratch offers you the most control over the ingredients that go into your food. We offer a simple recipe for a basic all-purpose flour blend on page 114 that uses gluten-free flours, along with suggestions for premixed flour blends if you're looking for a shortcut. Tip: Not all potentially contaminated products are foods. You could also inadvertently ingest gluten in products such as lipstick and lip balms, toothpaste, food additives, and medications or supplements that use gluten as a binding agent.

COMMERCIAL GLUTEN-FREE BREADS

You might prefer to make your own gluten-free breads, but if you don't have the time or inclination, you have options for buying gluten-free products. Ask friends and online communities for recommendations; check Web reviews and give items a try. Many products are offered by small companies that distribute nationally through health food stores and most regular supermarkets or make their wares available online. Check out products from Udi's Gluten Free Foods® (udisglutenfree.com), which carries everything from gluten-free hamburger and hotdog buns to bagels and English muffins, Rudi's (rudisglutenfree.com), and Food For Life® (foodforlife.com), which makes breads, English muffins® and tortillas. (By the way, don't assume that corn tortillas are gluten-free: Some brands may be produced using wheat, so check labels with care. Mission® corn tortillas, which are made from 100-percent corn, are labeled "gluten-free" on the package.) GFL Foods (glutenfreepitas.com) makes gluten-free pita bread, including a whole-grain version.

GLUTEN-FREE GRAINS

Instead of focusing on the foods you can't have, embrace what you can.

Because many grains are off-limits for people with celiac disease or gluten sensitivity, gluten-free grains are bedrock items in a gluten-free diet. They can sometimes be purchased in bulk at health food stores, though you should be wary of cross-contamination. Among the primary grains used in gluten-free cooking:

AMARANTH: Once a key grain in Aztec culture, it's loaded with fiber and protein and has a peppery flavor.

BUCKWHEAT: Not actually wheat, it's a plant whose seed contains a kernel called a groat that you can boil to eat as a hot cereal, roast for a side dish, or mill into a flour that can be used for pancakes. Buckwheat flour is also used to make some Asian noodles. Be cautious when buying buckwheat products. Check labels, because buckwheat is sometimes mixed with regular wheat.

CORN: Perhaps the most familiar grain to Americans, cornmeal and products like corn flour and cornstarch can often be substituted for wheat flour. Note that some cornstarch may contain wheat.

MILLET: Among the most ancient of grains and grown worldwide, millet is abundant in B vitamins and fiber, and contains moderate amounts of protein. It's best toasted, then boiled in water like rice.

QUINOA: Cultivated for thousands of years in South America, it's packed with protein and nutrients including B vitamins, iron, calcium, and fiber. Thorough rinsing removes the bitter coating.

RICE: It's familiar and versatile; opt for brown rice over white varieties. Because it's been stripped of its bran and germ, white rice (including the flavorful basmati) has only a shadow of the nutritive value of brown rice, even though it's often enriched. Brown rice generally takes longer to cook than white, but it's worth the wait, as

different varieties can introduce new flavors and textures.

TEFF: Though relatively new to Americans, it's a staple in parts of Africa. Featuring a sweet, nutty flavor, it's richer in calcium and iron than most other grains and also provides protein and fiber.

WILD RICE: A native North American grass (not technically a rice), it provides zinc, magnesium, and folate and makes an excellent side dish. Because of its relatively high cost and assertive, earthy flavor, it is often used in tandem with white or brown rice.

Hidden Gluten on Labels

When shopping, check labels on ready-made and processed foods such as soups, gravies, marinated meats, condiments, and more that contain emulsifiers, flavorings, hydrolyzed proteins, seasonings, stabilizers, and starches from unidentified sources. Here are some key words to look out for, as they may indicate that gluten is present. If in doubt, contact the company's customer-service center.

- Barley malt extract or barley malt flavoring
- Caramel coloring
- Dextrin
- Gravy
- Hydrolyzed wheat, plant, or vegetable proteins (HVP indicates hydrolyzed vegetable proteins)
- Malt (it's generally gluten-free if made from corn)
- Modified food starch/food starch (it's

generally gluten-free if made from rice, corn, or potato)
- Roux
- Soy sauce
- Textured vegetable protein (TVP)
- Vegetable gum (except the following gluten-free options: carob bean gum, cellulose gum, guar gum, locust bean gum, xanthan gum, gum arabic, gum aracia, gum tragacanth, and vegetable starch)
- Wheat flour or wheat gluten

Crustless Tomato-Ricotta Pie
(page 17)

1 Breakfasts & Brunches

Breakfast for most people is a one-note meal: cereal, played over and over. The fact that some staples of a traditional breakfast (including toast) aren't friendly to gluten-free eating is an opportunity in disguise.

Our wide array of gluten-free options provides a necessary burst of day-starting energy, but also breaks you out of a top-of-the-morning rut. For busy weekdays, fix-it-fast options include a smoothie you can whip up in little more time than it takes to pour milk on cereal. For weekends, prepare truly delectable kick-offs to your day like Potato-Crusted Quiche, which boasts a delicious shredded potato crust. Traditional a.m. ingredients like eggs and buckwheat create new gluten-free classics your grandma might envy, like pancakes, muffins, and banana bread. You'll even find a new take on an old tune with our hazelnut-honey granola—bake a batch in the oven and store it for a familiar cereal-and-milk opener to your day.

Pomegranate-Berry Smoothie 14

Banana-Peanut Butter Smoothie 14

Hazelnut & Fruit Granola 16

Crustless Tomato-Ricotta Pie 17

Huevos Rancheros 19

Potato-Crusted Quiche 20

Buckwheat Pancakes 22

Banana Bread 23

Morning Glory Muffins......... 25

POMEGRANATE-BERRY
Smoothie

Berries and pomegranates are loaded with heart-healthy antioxidants.

TOTAL TIME: 5 MINUTES   **MAKES:** 2 CUPS OR 1 SERVING

½ cup pomegranate juice, chilled

½ cup plain low-fat yogurt (see Tip)

1 cup frozen mixed berries

1 teaspoon honey

In blender, combine juice, yogurt, berries, and honey and blend until mixture is smooth. Pour into a tall glass.

TIP

Flavored yogurts may include additives that contain gluten. Opt for plain yogurt and add a sweetener, such as honey or agave nectar, or a flavoring, such as vanilla, if you like.

EACH SERVING: ABOUT 260 CALORIES | 6G PROTEIN | 52G CARBOHYDRATE | 2G TOTAL FAT (1G SATURATED) | 5G FIBER | 8MG CHOLESTEROL | 110MG SODIUM ♥ ☑

BANANA-PEANUT BUTTER
Smoothie

This yummy breakfast drink will keep you satisfied until lunchtime.

TOTAL TIME: 5 MINUTES   **MAKES:** 1½ CUPS OR 1 SERVING

1 small ripe banana, cut in half

½ cup soy milk

1 teaspoon natural creamy peanut butter

3 ice cubes

EACH SERVING: ABOUT 260 CALORIES | 6G PROTEIN | 52G CARBOHYDRATE | 2G TOTAL FAT (1G SATURATED) | 5G FIBER | 8MG CHOLESTEROL | 110MG SODIUM ♥ ☑

In blender, combine banana, soy milk, peanut butter, and ice and blend until mixture is smooth. Pour into a tall glass.

HAZELNUT & FRUIT
Granola

This scrumptious combination of toasty nuts, old-fashioned oats, and sweetly chewy dried fruit may be enjoyed straight from the container, spooned over plain yogurt, or with a splash of milk. Make sure to choose only oats that are labeled "gluten-free."

ACTIVE TIME: 10 MINUTES   **TOTAL TIME:** 55 MINUTES   **MAKES:** 10 CUPS OR 20 SERVINGS

½ cup honey or agave nectar

⅓ cup vegetable oil

1½ teaspoons vanilla extract (McCormick®, Spice Islands®, and Durkee® brands are gluten-free)

½ teaspoon ground cinnamon

4 cups old-fashioned gluten-free oats, such as Bob's Red Mill® brand, uncooked

1 cup flaked sweetened coconut

1 cup sliced almonds (4 ounces)

1 cup hazelnuts, chopped (4 ounces)

¼ cup flaxseeds

¼ cup pumpkin seeds (pepitas)

1 cup dried tart cherries

1 cup dried Calimyrna figs, stems removed, chopped

1 cup dried apricots, chopped

1   Preheat oven to 300°F.

2   In large bowl, whisk honey, oil, vanilla, and cinnamon until blended. Add oats, coconut, nuts, flaxseeds, and pumpkin seeds; stir until coated.

3   Divide mixture between two 15½" by 10½" jelly-roll pans; spread evenly.

4   Bake oat mixture until golden brown, 45 to 50 minutes, stirring twice during baking. Cool completely in pans on wire racks.

5   In large bowl, toss cooled oat mixture with cherries, figs, and apricots. Store in tightly covered container at room temperature for up to 1 week. For storage up to 3 weeks, and to keep granola crunchy, spoon oat mixture into one container and cherries, figs, and apricots into another. Mix together when ready to use.

EACH ½-CUP SERVING: ABOUT 270 CALORIES | 5G PROTEIN | 37G CARBOHYDRATE | 13G TOTAL FAT (2G SATURATED) | 5G FIBER | 0MG CHOLESTEROL | 5MG SODIUM ♥ ✿ ⬛

CRUSTLESS
Tomato-Ricotta Pie

Serve this delicious cross between a frittata and a quiche for brunch or dinner. Try this simple pie with a couple tablespoons of chopped fresh oregano or a handful of chopped fresh dill in place of the basil. For photo, see page 12.

ACTIVE TIME: 20 MINUTES   **TOTAL TIME:** 55 MINUTES   **MAKES:** 6 MAIN-DISH SERVINGS

1   container (15 ounces) part-skim ricotta cheese (Sargento® brand is gluten-free)

4   large eggs

¼   cup freshly grated Pecorino-Romano cheese

½   teaspoon salt

⅛   teaspoon ground black pepper

¼   cup low-fat (1%) milk

1   tablespoon cornstarch (see Tip)

½   cup loosely packed fresh basil leaves, chopped

½   cup loosely packed fresh mint leaves, chopped

1   pound ripe tomatoes (3 medium), thinly sliced

1   Preheat oven to 375°F. In large bowl, whisk ricotta, eggs, Romano, salt, and pepper until blended.

2   In measuring cup, stir milk and cornstarch until smooth; whisk into cheese mixture. Stir in basil and mint.

3   Pour mixture into nonstick 10-inch skillet with oven-safe handle. Arrange tomatoes on top, overlapping slices if necessary. Bake pie 35 to 40 minutes or until lightly browned on top, set around edge, and puffed at center. Let stand 5 minutes before serving.

TIP

Most cornstach is gluten-free, but read the label to make sure no wheat is added. Arrowroot can be used as a thickener instead, if you prefer, as can glutinous rice flour, potato flour, and many bean flours.

EACH SERVING: ABOUT 190 CALORIES | 15G PROTEIN | 10G CARBOHYDRATE | 10G TOTAL FAT (5G SATURATED) | 2G FIBER | 165MG CHOLESTEROL | 380MG SODIUM ☺

HUEVOS **Rancheros**

Fast and flavorful, these Mexican-inspired baked eggs are ideal for brunch. Spice up this dish with a drizzle of your favorite hot sauce. Use only corn tortillas made from 100-percent corn.

TOTAL TIME: 25 MINUTES   **MAKES:** 4 MAIN-DISH SERVINGS

- 1 tablespoon vegetable oil
- 1 medium onion, finely chopped
- 2 garlic cloves, crushed with garlic press
- 1 tablespoon chipotle sauce or other hot sauce, plus additional for serving
- 1 teaspoon ground cumin
- 1 can (28 ounces) whole tomatoes in juice, drained and chopped
- 1 can (15 to 19 ounces) black beans, rinsed and drained
- ¼ cup loosely packed fresh cilantro leaves, chopped
- ¼ teaspoon salt
- 1 tablespoon butter
- 4 large eggs
- 4 (6-inch) gluten-free corn tortillas, such as Chi-Chi's® or Mission® brands, warmed
- 1 avocado, sliced (optional)

1 In 4-quart saucepan, heat oil over medium heat until hot. Add onion and garlic and cook 8 minutes or until beginning to brown. Stir in chipotle sauce and cumin; cook 30 seconds, stirring. Add tomatoes; cover and cook 3 minutes to blend flavors, stirring occasionally. Stir in beans, half of cilantro, and salt; heat through, about 3 minutes, stirring occasionally.

2 Meanwhile, in 12-inch nonstick skillet, melt butter over medium heat. Crack eggs, one at a time, and drop into skillet. Cover skillet and cook eggs 4 to 5 minutes or until whites are set and yolks reach desired doneness.

3 Place tortillas on four dinner plates; top each with bean mixture and 1 egg. Sprinkle with remaining cilantro. Serve with avocado slices and additional hot sauce, if you like.

....

EACH SERVING: ABOUT 315 CALORIES | 15G PROTEIN | 42G CARBOHYDRATE | 12G TOTAL FAT (3G SATURATED) | 10G FIBER | 213MG CHOLESTEROL | 765MG SODIUM

😊 🌱

POTATO-CRUSTED
Quiche

A white flour and butter crust is not a requirement for quiche. Enjoy this clever gluten-free twist, which features a shredded potato crust flecked with green onions.

ACTIVE TIME: 20 MINUTES   **TOTAL TIME:** 40 MINUTES   **MAKES:** 4 MAIN-DISH SERVINGS

4   large eggs

1   large egg white

1²/3 cups low-fat (1%) milk

¼   teaspoon salt

⅛   teaspoon ground black pepper

4   ounces ham, cut into ¼-inch pieces

1½ pounds potatoes, peeled and shredded

2   green onions, chopped

2   tablespoons olive oil

2   ounces Swiss cheese, shredded (Kraft® Natural Shredded Swiss Cheese is gluten-free)

2   plum tomatoes, thinly sliced

fresh flat-leaf parsley leaves and snipped fresh chives, for garnish

1 Preheat oven to 375°F.

2 In large bowl, with wire whisk, blend eggs, egg white, milk, ⅛ teaspoon salt, and pepper. Stir in ham.

3 Place potatoes in large fine-mesh sieve. With hands, squeeze out as much liquid as possible. Transfer to large bowl and toss with green onions and remaining ⅛ teaspoon salt.

4 Heat 12-inch well-seasoned plain or enamel-coated cast-iron skillet on medium-high until hot. Add oil and heat until very hot, brushing to evenly coat bottom and sides. Add potatoes; with rubber spatula, quickly spread in thin, even layer over bottom and up sides to rim, gently pressing potatoes against pan to form crust. Patch holes by using spatula to spread potatoes over them. Cook 3 minutes or until browned. Pour in egg mixture, then sprinkle Swiss cheese evenly over top.

5 Bake 15 to 20 minutes or until a knife inserted in center comes out clean. Decoratively arrange tomato slices on top. Garnish with parsley and chives. Use thin spatula to release sides of crust from pan, then cut into wedges to serve.

EACH SERVING: ABOUT 425 CALORIES | 23G PROTEIN | 39G CARBOHYDRATE | 20G TOTAL FAT (6G SATURATED) | 4G FIBER | 253MG CHOLESTEROL | 660MG SODIUM ☺

BUCKWHEAT
Pancakes

Buckwheat flour adds a wonderful nutty flavor to these buttermilk pancakes. Because buckwheat contains more of the whole grain, store tightly covered in the refrigerator to keep it from going rancid.

TOTAL TIME: 30 MINUTES   **MAKES:** ABOUT 14 PANCAKES

½ cup All-Purpose Flour Blend (page 114) or gluten-free all-purpose flour

½ cup buckwheat flour

1 tablespoon sugar

2 teaspoons baking powder

½ teaspoon baking soda

¼ teaspoon salt

1¼ cups buttermilk

3 tablespoons butter, melted and cooled

1 large egg, lightly beaten

vegetable oil, for brushing pan

1 In large bowl, combine flours, sugar, baking powder, baking soda, and salt. Add buttermilk, butter, and egg; stir just until flour is moistened.
2 Heat griddle or 12-inch skillet over medium-low heat until drop of water sizzles when sprinkled on hot surface; brush lightly with oil. Pour batter by scant ¼ cups onto hot griddle, making 2 or 3 pancakes at a time. Cook until tops are bubbly and edges look dry, 2 to 3 minutes. With wide spatula, turn pancakes and cook until undersides brown, 2 to 3 minutes longer. Transfer to platter; keep warm.
3 Repeat with remaining batter, brushing griddle with more oil as needed.

EACH PANCAKE: ABOUT 80 CALORIES | 2G PROTEIN | 8G CARBOHYDRATE | 4G TOTAL FAT (2G SATURATED) | 1G FIBER | 21MG CHOLESTEROL | 215MG SODIUM

BANANA **Bread**

Studded with walnuts and bursting with banana flavor,
this bread is so moist, you'd never guess it's gluten-free.

ACTIVE TIME: 25 MINUTES   TOTAL TIME: 1 HOUR 25 MINUTES   MAKES: 1 LARGE LOAF (16 SLICES)

1¾ cups All-Purpose Flour Blend (page 114)
   or gluten-free all-purpose flour

1½ teaspoons baking powder

¾ teaspoon baking soda

½ teaspoon xanthan gum (see Tip)

¼ teaspoon salt

½ cup butter (1 stick), softened

¾ cup packed light brown sugar

2 large eggs

1 teaspoon vanilla extract (McCormick®,
   Spice Islands®, and Durkee® are gluten-free)

1½ cups mashed ripe bananas (3 to 4 large)

½ cup walnuts, chopped

1 Preheat oven to 350°F. Grease 9" by 5" metal loaf pan. In medium bowl, whisk together flour blend, baking powder, baking soda, xanthan gum, and salt.

2 In large bowl, with mixer on medium speed, beat butter and brown sugar until light and creamy. Beat in eggs, one at a time. Beat in vanilla. Reduce speed to low; beat in flour mixture alternately with bananas, beginning and ending with flour mixture, scraping bowl occasionally. Stir in walnuts. Scrape batter into prepared pan.

3 Bake 50 to 60 minutes or until toothpick inserted in center of loaf comes out clean. Cool in pan on wire rack 10 minutes. Remove from pan and cool completely on wire rack.

TIP

Despite its alien-sounding name, xanthan gum is a natural sugar derived from corn. This 100-percent gluten-free thickener is available at most health-food stores.

EACH SLICE: ABOUT 195 CALORIES | 2G PROTEIN | 28G CARBOHYDRATE | 9G TOTAL FAT (4G SATURATED) | 2G FIBER | 38MG CHOLESTEROL | 210MG SODIUM 🍱 ❤

MORNING GLORY
Muffins

Here is the ultimate breakfast muffin: a carrot cake–like batter dressed up with pecans, dried fruit, and a shredded Granny Smith apple to add a little tartness.

ACTIVE TIME: 20 MINUTES   **TOTAL TIME:** 45 MINUTES   **MAKES:** 12 MUFFINS

1½ cups All-Purpose Flour Blend (page 114) or gluten-free all-purpose flour

1½ teaspoons ground cinnamon

1 teaspoon baking powder

1 teaspoon baking soda

1 teaspoon xanthan gum (see Tip, page 23)

½ teaspoon salt

⅓ cup packed brown sugar

⅓ cup granulated sugar

2 large eggs

⅓ cup canola oil

1 cup packaged shredded carrot

1 Granny Smith apple, peeled, cored, and shredded

½ cup pecans, chopped

½ cup dried fruit bits or golden raisins

1 Preheat oven to 375°F. Line 12-cup muffin pan with paper liners.

2 In medium bowl, combine flour blend, cinnamon, baking powder, baking soda, xanthan gum, and salt. In large bowl, stir together brown sugar, granulated sugar, eggs, and oil. Add flour mixture and stir until blended. Stir in carrot, apple, pecans, and dried fruit.

3 Spoon batter into muffin-pan cups. Bake 20 to 27 minutes or until toothpick inserted in center of muffins comes out clean. Remove to wire rack to cool.

EACH SERVING: ABOUT 225 CALORIES | 3G PROTEIN | 33G CARBOHYDRATE | 10G TOTAL FAT (1G SATURATED) | 2G FIBER | 31MG CHOLESTEROL | 268MG SODIUM ♥ 🗄

Salad Niçoise
(page 36)

2 Hearty Sandwiches & Salads

These recipes deliver protein for a midday boost of slow-burning energy along with faster-acting carbohydrates. And many of these offerings, like Mango Chicken Lettuce Cups or Open-Faced Smoked Salmon Sandwiches, can be packed in insulated containers so you can whip them out when your busy schedule allows.

For recipes that call for the familiar, hearty presence of bread, you can choose to buy gluten-free products or make your own with our Homemade Sandwich Bread recipe, which not only provides everyday lunch foundations but the basis for breadcrumbs that you can use in casseroles and other dishes. Beyond their delicious taste and appealing presentation, the vegetable- and grain-based salad recipes here keep you full throughout the day, while also providing a number of dietary elements that are especially important to people on a gluten-free diet, like the ample fiber in the Warm Quinoa Salad with Toasted Almonds or the Lentil Salad with Shrimp, Apples & Mint.

Rice & Bean Burgers 28

Homemade Sandwich Bread 29

Curried Chicken Pitas 30

Open-Faced Smoked Salmon Sandwiches 32

Mango Chicken Lettuce Cups 34

Salad Niçoise 36

Six-Bean Salad with Tomato Vinaigrette 37

Lentil Salad with Shrimp, Apples & Mint 39

Warm Quinoa Salad with Toasted Almonds 40

RICE & BEAN
Burgers

Forget the bun and enjoy these mini "burger" patties wrapped up in flavored tortillas with a refreshing tahini-lemon yogurt sauce.

TOTAL TIME: 20 MINUTES   **MAKES:** 4 MAIN-DISH SERVINGS

1   lemon

1   container (6 ounces) plain low-fat yogurt

4   tablespoons well-stirred tahini (sesame paste)

3/4 teaspoon salt

1   package (8 to 9 ounces) precooked brown rice

1   can (15 to 19 ounces) garbanzo beans

1   garlic clove, crushed with garlic press

1/2 teaspoon fennel seeds

nonstick cooking spray

4   burrito-size (10-inch) gluten-free spinach or red chile tortillas, such as Sandwich Petals brand

2   carrots, peeled and shredded

2   ripe plum tomatoes, thinly sliced

1   Kirby (pickling) cucumber, not peeled, thinly sliced

1 Prepare outdoor grill for direct grilling over medium heat.

2 Meanwhile, from lemon, grate 1½ teaspoons peel and squeeze 2 tablespoons juice. In small serving bowl, stir lemon juice, yogurt, 2 tablespoons tahini, and ½ teaspoon salt until blended. Set yogurt sauce aside. (Makes about ¾ cup.)

3 Prepare rice in microwave oven as label directs. Set aside.

4 Reserve ¼ cup liquid from beans. Rinse beans and drain well. In medium bowl, combine beans, lemon peel, garlic, fennel seeds, remaining ¼ teaspoon salt, remaining 2 tablespoons tahini, and reserved bean liquid. With potato masher, coarsely mash bean mixture until well blended but still lumpy. Add rice and continue to mash just until blended.

5 Shape bean mixture into eight 1-inch-thick burgers. Coat both sides of burgers with cooking spray. Place burgers on very hot grill rack. Cook until well browned on the outside, 10 to 12 minutes, turning burgers over once.

6 To serve, place 2 burgers in center of each tortilla; top with sauce, carrots, tomatoes, and cucumber. Fold opposite sides of each tortilla over filling, then fold ends over to form a package.

EACH SERVING: ABOUT 465 CALORIES | 17G PROTEIN | 70G CARBOHYDRATE | 13G TOTAL FAT (2G SATURATED) | 10G FIBER | 3MG CHOLESTEROL | 588MG SODIUM

HOMEMADE
Sandwich Bread

Banish dry, crumbly (not to mention costly!) storebought gluten-free bread with this delicious loaf. Bake it in multiples; the loaves can be wrapped tightly and frozen for later use.

ACTIVE TIME: 25 MINUTES   **TOTAL TIME:** 1 HOUR 10 MINUTES PLUS RISING AND COOLING
MAKES: 1 LARGE LOAF (16 SLICES)

- 1½ cups warm water (105°F to 115°F)
- 1 package active dry yeast
- 2 tablespoons packed brown sugar
- 2 cups All-Purpose Flour Blend (page 114) or gluten-free all-purpose flour
- 1 cup brown rice flour
- ½ cup millet flour
- ¼ cup instant nonfat dry milk powder
- 4 teaspoons xanthan gum (see Tip, page 23)
- 2 teaspoons baking powder
- 1 teaspoon salt
- 2 large eggs, at room temperature
- 4 tablespoons butter, melted
- 1 teaspoon apple cider vinegar

1 In small bowl, combine ¼ cup warm water, yeast, and 1 teaspoon brown sugar; stir and let stand 5 minutes, or until foamy.

2 In medium bowl, whisk remaining sugar, flour blend, brown rice flour, millet flour, milk powder, xanthan gum, baking powder, and salt.

3 In bowl of stand mixer fitted with paddle attachment (not dough hook), combine yeast mixture, remaining 1¼ cups warm water, eggs, butter, and vinegar. Beat on low speed until blended. Add flour mixture and beat on low speed until combined. Increase speed to medium and beat for 4 minutes, scraping sides of bowl occasionally.

4 Spray 9" by 5" metal loaf pan with cooking spray. Scrape batter into prepared pan and spread to fill pan, mounding batter slightly in center. Cover pan loosely with greased plastic wrap. Let sit in warm place until batter rises ½ inch above pan sides, 1 to 2 hours.

5 Preheat oven to 375°F. Bake 45 to 55 minutes or until loaf is well browned and instant-read thermometer registers 210°F when inserted in center of loaf, loosely tenting bread with foil if surface browns too much. Remove from pan and let cool completely on wire rack.

EACH SLICE: ABOUT 155 CALORIES | 3G PROTEIN | 27G CARBOHYDRATE | 7G TOTAL FAT (3G SATURATED) | 2G FIBER | 29MG CHOLESTEROL | 257MG SODIUM

CURRIED CHICKEN
Pitas

This curry-spiced chicken salad packs extra sweet flavor with the addition of cantaloupe. Serve it on toasted pita or atop peppery watercress or crisp romaine lettuce for a light and casual summer meal.

TOTAL TIME: 20 MINUTES   **MAKES:** 4 SANDWICHES

- ¼ cup packed fresh cilantro leaves, finely chopped
- ¼ cup reduced-fat sour cream (Cabot®, Daisy®, and Breakstone's™ brands are gluten-free)
- 2 tablespoons low-fat mayonnaise
- 1 tablespoon fresh lime juice
- 1 teaspoon grated, peeled fresh ginger
- ¼ teaspoon curry powder
- ¼ teaspoon ground coriander
- ⅛ teaspoon salt
- 2 cups chopped, cooked chicken breast meat
- 5 radishes, cut into ¼-inch-thick half-moons
- 1½ cups (8 ounces) chopped cantaloupe
- ¼ small red onion, finely chopped
- 3 tablespoons roasted cashews, chopped
- 4 gluten-free pita breads, such as GFL Foods brand, each toasted and cut into halves

1 In small bowl, whisk cilantro, sour cream, mayonnaise, lime juice, ginger, curry powder, coriander, and salt until well blended. If making ahead, cover and refrigerate up to 1 day.
2 In bowl, combine chicken, radishes, cantaloupe, and onion. If making ahead, cover and refrigerate up to 1 day. To serve, toss chicken mixture with half of dressing. Sprinkle with cashews. Spoon on top of pita pieces and serve with remaining dressing alongside.

EACH SERVING: ABOUT 375 CALORIES | 24G PROTEIN | 47G CARBOHYDRATE | 10G TOTAL FAT (3G SATURATED) | 2G FIBER | 67MG CHOLESTEROL | 640MG SODIUM

OPEN-FACED SMOKED SALMON
Sandwiches

Turn a brunch treat into an elegant luncheon, swapping the gluten-loaded bagel for the chewy goodness of a gluten-free whole-grain bread.

TOTAL TIME: 20 MINUTES   **MAKES:** 4 SANDWICHES

1   lemon

⅓   cup (3 ounces) light cream cheese, softened (Philadelphia™ brand is gluten-free)

1   stalk celery, finely chopped

½   carrot, peeled and finely shredded

2   tablespoons drained capers

2   tablespoons chopped green onions

2   teaspoons chopped fresh dill, plus sprigs for garnish

4   thin slices (4 ounces) gluten-free whole-grain bread or Homemade Sandwich Bread (page 29)

1   package (4 ounces) sliced smoked salmon

1 From lemon, grate 1 teaspoon peel and squeeze 1 tablespoon juice. In medium bowl, combine lemon peel and juice, cream cheese, celery, carrot, capers, green onions, and chopped dill. Stir to blend.

2 Spread cream cheese mixture on one side of each bread slice; top with smoked salmon. Cut each sandwich into quarters; garnish with dill sprigs to serve.

EACH SERVING: ABOUT 185 CALORIES | 10G PROTEIN | 21G CARBOHYDRATE | 7G TOTAL FAT (4G SATURATED) | 2G FIBER | 37MG CHOLESTEROL | 640MG SODIUM

MANGO CHICKEN
Lettuce Cups

Skip the bread and wrap these speedy, no-cook chicken wraps in crisp lettuce leaves instead. Mango, fresh mint, and jicama add a Latin-American zing.

TOTAL TIME: 20 MINUTES   **MAKES:** 4 MAIN-DISH SERVINGS

1   large ripe mango, peeled and chopped

1   cup finely chopped jicama

½   cup packed fresh mint leaves, finely chopped

¼   cup fresh lime juice

2   tablespoons extra-virgin olive oil

½   teaspoon Asian chili sauce (Sriracha), plus more to taste

¼   teaspoon salt

3   cups coarsely shredded chicken meat (from ½ rotisserie chicken)

12   Boston lettuce leaves

1   In large bowl, combine mango, jicama, mint, lime juice, oil, chili sauce, and salt. Toss to combine. If making ahead, cover bowl and refrigerate mixture up to overnight.

2   To serve, add chicken to mango mixture; toss to combine. Place ⅓ cup chicken mixture in each lettuce leaf.

EACH SERVING: ABOUT 325 CALORIES | 32G PROTEIN | 17G CARBOHYDRATE | 15G TOTAL FAT (3G SATURATED) | 4G FIBER | 94MG CHOLESTEROL | 400MG SODIUM

Salad NIÇOISE

This classic French composed salad is the perfect entrée for
a ladies' lunch or light dinner. For photo, see page 26.

ACTIVE TIME: 30 MINUTES   **TOTAL TIME:** 1 HOUR 5 MINUTES   **MAKES:** 6 MAIN-DISH SERVINGS

⅓ cup loosely packed fresh parsley leaves, chopped

¼ cup red wine vinegar

3 tablespoons olive oil

1 teaspoon Dijon mustard (Grey Poupon® and Maille® are gluten-free)

¼ teaspoon salt

¼ teaspoon ground black pepper

1 pound small red potatoes

6 large eggs

½ pound green beans, trimmed and cut crosswise in half

1 bag (5 ounces) mixed baby greens (8 cups loosely packed)

½ English (seedless) cucumber, thinly sliced

1 can (12 ounces) solid white tuna in water, drained

3 medium tomatoes, cut into wedges

½ cup (3 ounces) niçoise olives

1 Into small bowl, measure parsley, vinegar, oil, mustard, salt, and pepper. Mix vinaigrette with wire whisk or fork until blended; set aside.

2 In 3-quart saucepan, place unpeeled potatoes and enough *water* to cover; heat to boiling over high heat. Reduce heat to low; simmer 10 to 12 minutes or until potatoes are fork-tender.

3 Meanwhile, in 2-quart saucepan, place eggs and enough *cold water* to cover by 1 inch; heat to boiling over high heat. Remove saucepan from heat and cover tightly; let stand 15 minutes. Pour off hot water; run cold water over eggs to cool. Remove shells and cut each egg into wedges.

4 When potatoes are done, with slotted spoon, transfer to colander to drain. To same water in saucepan, add beans; heat to boiling over high heat. Reduce heat to low; simmer 5 to 10 minutes or until tender-crisp. Drain beans; rinse with cold running water to stop cooking; drain again.

5 In large bowl, toss greens with half of vinaigrette. Place greens on large platter. Cut each potato in half or quarters if large; transfer to platter with greens. Arrange beans, eggs, cucumber, tuna, tomatoes, and olives in separate piles on same platter; drizzle with remaining vinaigrette.

EACH SERVING: ABOUT 315 CALORIES | 22G PROTEIN | 24G CARBOHYDRATE | 15G TOTAL FAT (3G SATURATED) | 4G FIBER | 233MG CHOLESTEROL | 515MG SODIUM
☺ ♥

Six-Bean Salad
WITH TOMATO VINAIGRETTE

This salad is a tasty powerhouse of protein, iron, and bone-building vitamin K. The tomato dressing contributes a zesty finish.

ACTIVE TIME: 20 MINUTES   **TOTAL TIME:** 26 MINUTES PLUS CHILLING   **MAKES:** 18 SIDE-DISH SERVINGS

1   teaspoon salt

8   ounces green beans, trimmed and cut into 1-inch pieces

8   ounces wax beans, trimmed and cut into 1-inch pieces

1   can (15 to 19 ounces) garbanzo beans

1   can (15 to 19 ounces) black beans or black soybeans

1   can (15 to 19 ounces) red kidney beans

1½ cups (half a 16-ounce bag) frozen shelled edamame (green soybeans), thawed

TOMATO VINAIGRETTE

1   small ripe tomato (4 ounces), coarsely chopped

1   small shallot, coarsely chopped

¼   cup olive oil

2   tablespoons red wine vinegar

1   tablespoon Dijon mustard (Grey Poupon® and Maille® are gluten-free)

½   teaspoon salt

¼   teaspoon ground black pepper

1 In 12-inch skillet, heat *1 inch water* with salt to boiling over high heat. Add green and wax beans; return water to a boil. Reduce heat to low; simmer until beans are tender-crisp, 6 to 8 minutes. Drain beans. Rinse with cold running water to stop cooking; drain again. Transfer beans to large serving bowl.

2 While green and wax beans are cooking, rinse and drain garbanzo, black, and kidney beans. Add canned beans and edamame to bowl with green and wax beans.

3 Prepare Tomato Vinaigrette: In blender, combine tomato, shallot, oil, vinegar, mustard, salt, and pepper. Blend until smooth.

4 Add vinaigrette to beans in bowl. Toss until beans are evenly coated. Cover and refrigerate at least 1 hour to blend flavors or up to 8 hours.

....

EACH SERVING: ABOUT 130 CALORIES | 7G PROTEIN | 17G CARBOHYDRATE | 4G TOTAL FAT (0G SATURATED) | 6G FIBER | 0MG CHOLESTEROL | 230MG SODIUM

☺ ♥ ☻ ▭

Lentil Salad
WITH SHRIMP, APPLES & MINT

This heart-healthy salad is chock-full of fiber, thanks to crisp Golden Delicious apples and a lentil base.

ACTIVE TIME: 15 MINUTES　**TOTAL TIME:** 50 MINUTES　**MAKES:** 4 MAIN-DISH SERVINGS

3	tablespoons olive oil
3	tablespoons cider vinegar
1½	teaspoons salt
¼	teaspoon ground black pepper
1	pound fresh or frozen (thawed) shelled and deveined medium shrimp
1	cup lentils
6	cups water
1	small onion (4 to 6 ounces), chopped
½	cup loosely packed fresh mint leaves, chopped
1	Golden Delicious apple, not peeled, cored, and cut into ½-inch chunks
1	stalk celery, thinly sliced

1 In small bowl, whisk oil, vinegar, salt, and pepper. Spoon 2 tablespoons dressing into medium bowl. Add shrimp; toss to coat.

2 In colander, rinse lentils with cold water and discard any stones or shriveled lentils. In 4-quart saucepan, combine lentils, water, onion, and 2 tablespoons mint; heat to boiling over high heat. Reduce heat to low; cover and simmer 20 to 30 minutes or until lentils are tender but still hold shape. Drain well.

3 Meanwhile, heat 12-inch skillet over medium-high heat until hot. Add shrimp with any dressing and cook 4 to 5 minutes or until shrimp turn opaque. Remove from heat; stir in 1 tablespoon mint.

4 Stir shrimp, apple, celery, remaining mint, and remaining dressing into lentils. Serve warm.

EACH SERVING: ABOUT 410 CALORIES | 37G PROTEIN | 37G CARBOHYDRATE | 13G TOTAL FAT (2G SATURATED) | 17G FIBER | 172MG CHOLESTEROL | 475MG SODIUM

Warm Quinoa Salad
WITH TOASTED ALMONDS

Often called a supergrain because it contains all eight essential amino acids, quinoa is considered a complete protein. Toasting quinoa brings out its delicate nutty flavor and reduces its bitter aftertaste.

ACTIVE TIME: 5 MINUTES   **TOTAL TIME:** 30 MINUTES   **MAKES:** 5 SIDE-DISH SERVINGS

1½ cups quinoa, thoroughly rinsed

2½ cups plus 1 tablespoon water

½ teaspoon salt

2 tablespoons reduced-sodium tamari, such as San-J™ brand

1 tablespoon rice vinegar

1 teaspoon Asian sesame oil

1 teaspoon grated, peeled fresh ginger

2 green onions, thinly sliced diagonally

¼ cup sliced natural almonds, toasted

1 In 12-inch dry skillet, toast quinoa over medium heat until fragrant and golden, about 5 minutes, stirring frequently.

2 Stir 2½ cups water and salt into toasted quinoa; heat to boiling over high heat. Reduce heat to low; cover and simmer until all water is absorbed, 15 to 17 minutes.

3 Meanwhile, in small bowl, stir together tamari, vinegar, oil, ginger, green onions, and remaining 1 tablespoon water.

4 Transfer quinoa to large serving bowl. Stir in tamari mixture until quinoa is evenly coated. Sprinkle with toasted almonds to serve.

EACH SERVING: ABOUT 305 CALORIES | 9G PROTEIN | 38G CARBOHYDRATE | 7G TOTAL FAT (1G SATURATED) | 4G FIBER | 0MG CHOLESTEROL | 460MG SODIUM ♥ ♥

Coq au Riesling
(page 52)

3 Soups & Stews

The embodiment of comfort food, a bowl of soup or stew brings to mind images of home and hearth that seem both modern and timeless. In fact, with their bounty of fresh ingredients and simplicity of presentation, these dishes are thought to be as old as cooking itself; variations on the put-it-in-the-pot theme can be found in virtually every culture. You'll get a sense of that cultural variety from a number of the recipes here, including Vietnamese Rice Noodle Soup, Fish Stew, and Pork Posole.

We haven't forgotten the comfort aspect, either: You'll find longtime favorites like Tomato Soup with a twist of Tofu-Parmesan Croutons and our healthy version of Beef Burgundy. One note: Canned broths may be a source of hidden gluten, so be sure to check labels (or use the gluten-free brands). Pull up a chair—soup's on!

Chilled Corn &
Bacon Soup 44

Tomato Soup with Tofu-
Parmesan Croutons 46

Mixed Vegetable
Minestrone 47

Fish Stew 49

Healthy Makeover
Beef Burgundy 50

Coq au Riesling 52

Valentine's Day
Red Chili 53

Pork Posole 54

Vietnamese Rice Noodle
Soup 55

CHILLED CORN & BACON **Soup**

Light but lush—thickened with late-season corn (rather than flour), low-fat milk, and a Yukon Gold potato—this refreshing farm-stand soup is summer's answer to cold-weather chowders.

ACTIVE TIME: 25 MINUTES   TOTAL TIME: 35 MINUTES PLUS CHILLING   MAKES: 4 MAIN-DISH SERVINGS

4   slices thick-cut bacon (Smith's®, Hormel™, and Oscar Meyer® offer gluten-free options; see Tip), cut into 1/2-inch pieces

1   large shallot, finely chopped

3   cups corn kernels cut from cobs (about 6 ears)

1   large Yukon Gold potato (8 ounces), peeled and shredded

1/8   teaspoon smoked paprika, plus additional for garnish

2/3   cup water

4   cups low-fat (1%) milk

1/8   teaspoon salt

1/8   teaspoon ground black pepper

1/4   cup packed fresh cilantro leaves

1 In 12-inch skillet, cook bacon over medium heat 6 to 8 minutes or until crisp and browned. With slotted spoon, transfer to paper towels to drain. If making ahead, cover and refrigerate up to overnight.

2 Drain and discard all but 1 tablespoon fat from skillet. Add shallot and cook over medium heat 2 minutes or until golden and tender, stirring occasionally. Add 2½ cups corn, potato, and paprika. Cook 2 minutes, stirring, then add water and cook 7 minutes or until liquid evaporates and vegetables are tender.

3 Remove skillet from heat and transfer corn mixture to blender. Add milk and salt and puree until mixture is very smooth. Cover and refrigerate until soup is cold, at least 3 hours and up to overnight.

4 To serve, divide among serving bowls. Top with bacon, pepper, cilantro, and remaining ½ cup corn. Garnish with paprika.

> **TIP**
>
> Some bacons contain gluten; it is primarily used as a filler. Start with the brands we recommend above and read labels with care.

EACH SERVING: ABOUT 375 CALORIES | 17G PROTEIN | 54G CARBOHYDRATE | 12G TOTAL FAT (5G SATURATED) | 5G FIBER | 23MG CHOLESTEROL | 750MG SODIUM

Tomato Soup
WITH TOFU-PARMESAN CROUTONS

This luscious tomato soup is garnished with a surprise: baked croutons made from Parmesan-encrusted tofu. Use a store-bought gluten-free bread—preferably whole-grain—or a day-old slice of our Homemade Sandwich Bread (page 29) to make the crumbs.

ACTIVE TIME: 15 MINUTES   **TOTAL TIME:** 40 MINUTES   **MAKES:** 4 MAIN-DISH SERVINGS

1   tablespoon olive oil

1   cup packaged shredded carrots

1   small onion (4 to 6 ounces), finely chopped

2   garlic cloves, crushed with garlic press

2   cans (28 ounces each) whole tomatoes in juice

1   cup water

½   teaspoon salt

¼   teaspoon ground black pepper

1   package (14 ounces) firm tofu, drained

1   slice gluten-free whole-grain bread, coarsely grated into crumbs

½   cup freshly grated Parmesan cheese

1 In 6-quart saucepot, heat oil over medium-high heat. Add carrots, onion, and garlic and cook, covered, 5 to 7 minutes or until vegetables begin to brown, stirring occasionally.

2 Stir in tomatoes with their juice, water, salt, and pepper, breaking up tomatoes with spoon; heat to boiling. Reduce heat to medium-low; partially cover and simmer 20 minutes.

3 Meanwhile, preheat broiler for making croutons. Cut tofu into 8 slices. Place slices between layers of paper towels and gently press to extract excess moisture. In bowl, combine bread crumbs and Parmesan. Spray cookie sheet with nonstick cooking spray. Arrange tofu on cookie sheet; sprinkle with crumb mixture. Place cookie sheet in broiler, 5 to 6 inches from source of heat, and broil tofu 5 to 8 minutes or until browned.

4 To serve, with potato masher, crush tomatoes in soup. Top each serving of soup with 2 croutons.

EACH SERVING: ABOUT 270 CALORIES | 16G PROTEIN | 31G CARBOHYDRATE | 12G TOTAL FAT (3G SATURATED) | 6G FIBER | 7MG CHOLESTEROL | 1,125MG SODIUM
☺ ☻

MIXED VEGETABLE
Minestrone

Tubetti pasta is available gluten-free, but you can also substitute larger gluten-free noodles broken into small pieces prior to cooking.

ACTIVE TIME: 18 MINUTES   TOTAL TIME: 40 MINUTES   MAKES: 6 MAIN-DISH SERVINGS

2 tablespoons olive oil

1 medium onion (6 to 8 ounces), finely chopped

2 garlic cloves, crushed with garlic press

3/4 teaspoon salt

3/4 teaspoon ground black pepper

1 can (28 ounces) diced tomatoes

4 cups water

1 pound carrots, peeled and cut into 1/2-inch pieces

1 small bunch (12 ounces) Swiss chard, stems discarded, leaves thinly sliced (5 1/2 cups)

8 ounces green beans, trimmed and cut into 1-inch pieces

1 1/2 cups frozen shelled edamame (green soybeans)

1 can (15 ounces) low-sodium white kidney (cannellini) beans, rinsed and drained

1 cup gluten-free tubetti or other short pasta, such as Sam Mills® or Le Veneziane® brands

1/2 cup plus 6 tablespoons freshly grated Parmesan cheese

1 In 5- to 6-quart saucepot, heat 1 tablespoon oil over medium heat until hot. Stir in onion, garlic, 1/2 teaspoon salt, and 1/2 teaspoon pepper. Cover and cook 4 to 5 minutes or until tender. Add tomatoes and water. Heat to boiling over medium-high heat. Add carrots; cover and cook 10 minutes, stirring occasionally. Add chard and green beans; cook 6 minutes or until beans are just tender, stirring occasionally. Add edamame and white beans; cook 5 minutes or until edamame are just cooked through. (Can be prepared to this point up to 2 days ahead; transfer to airtight container and refrigerate. Reheat before continuing with recipe.)

2 Meanwhile, cook pasta as label directs. Drain well and stir into saucepot with soup. Stir in 1/2 cup Parmesan and remaining 1/4 teaspoon each salt and pepper. Ladle into six soup bowls. Top each portion with 1 tablespoon Parmesan and 1/2 teaspoon oil.

EACH SERVING: ABOUT 575 CALORIES | 38G PROTEIN | 63G CARBOHYDRATE | 21G TOTAL FAT (3G SATURATED) | 17G FIBER | 7MG CHOLESTEROL | 775MG SODIUM

♥ 🌱 🍲

FISH **Stew**

Much like a traditional French Bouillabaisse, this light and tasty stew features a delicate fennel flavor and tender pieces of fresh seafood.

ACTIVE TIME: 20 MINUTES   **TOTAL TIME:** 35 MINUTES   **MAKES:** 4 MAIN-DISH SERVINGS

1   tablespoon olive oil

1   small onion (4 to 6 ounces), finely chopped

1   small red pepper, chopped

1   large garlic clove, crushed with garlic press

½   teaspoon fennel seeds

⅛   teaspoon crushed red pepper

¾   cup dry white wine

1   can (28 ounces) whole tomatoes in juice, coarsely chopped

1   cup water

½   teaspoon salt

12   ounces cod, hake, or Alaskan pollock fillet, cut into 2-inch pieces

1   pound blue mussels, scrubbed and beards removed (see Tip)

8   ounces fresh or frozen (thawed) shelled and deveined medium shrimp

½   cup loosely packed fresh basil leaves, sliced

1 In 5- to 6-quart Dutch oven, heat oil over medium heat. Add onion and chopped pepper and cook 6 to 8 minutes or until tender. Add garlic, fennel seeds, and crushed red pepper and cook 1 minute longer, stirring. Add wine; heat to boiling.

2 Stir in tomatoes with their juice, water, and salt; heat to boiling over high heat.

3 Add cod, mussels, and shrimp; return to boiling. Reduce heat to low; cover. Simmer 8 to 9 minutes or until cod and shrimp turn opaque and mussels open. Discard any mussels that have not opened after 9 minutes. Sprinkle stew with basil to serve.

TIP

Most markets carry blue mussels. They have bluish-black shells and are harvested wild or cultivated (the cultivated type may not have beards). To debeard a mussel, grasp the hairlike threads with your thumb and forefinger and pull them away from the shell. Once you have removed the beards, cook the mussels within the hour, as they will die quickly and spoil.

EACH SERVING: ABOUT 265 CALORIES | 37G PROTEIN | 15G CARBOHYDRATE | 6G TOTAL FAT (1G SATURATED) | 3G FIBER | 147MG CHOLESTEROL | 805MG SODIUM ☺ ♥

HEALTHY MAKEOVER
Beef Burgundy

We dropped the bacon—a classic ingredient in a French-style beef stew—but couldn't bear to trade juicy beef chuck for tougher round, even though chuck is a bit fattier. Instead, we added lots more vegetables, like fresh mushrooms, carrots, and frozen peas, to stretch the meat and ramp up the nutritional value.

ACTIVE TIME: 45 MINUTES   **TOTAL TIME:** 2 HOURS 15 MINUTES   **MAKES:** 8 MAIN-DISH SERVINGS

1	tablespoon olive oil
2	pounds boneless beef chuck, trimmed of fat and cut into 1½-inch chunks
3	large carrots (4 ounces each), cut into 1-inch pieces
3	garlic cloves, crushed with side of chef's knife
1	large onion (12 ounces), cut into 1-inch pieces
2	tablespoons All-Purpose Flour Blend (page 114) or gluten-free all-purpose flour
2	tablespoons tomato paste
¾	teaspoon salt
½	teaspoon ground black pepper
2	cups dry red wine
4	sprigs fresh thyme
2	packages (10 ounces each) mushrooms, cut in half
1	bag (16 ounces) frozen peas

1 In 5- to 6-quart Dutch oven, heat oil over medium-high heat until hot. Pat beef dry with paper towels. Add beef, in two batches, and cook 5 to 6 minutes per batch or until well browned on all sides. With slotted spoon, transfer beef to medium bowl. Preheat oven to 325°F.

2 To drippings in Dutch oven, add carrots, garlic, and onion and cook 10 minutes or until vegetables are browned and tender, stirring occasionally. Stir in flour blend, tomato paste, salt, and pepper; cook 1 minute, stirring. Add wine and heat to boiling, stirring until browned bits are loosened from bottom of Dutch oven.

3 Return meat and any meat juices in bowl to Dutch oven. Add thyme and mushrooms; heat to boiling. Cover and bake 1½ hours or until meat is fork-tender, stirring once. Discard thyme sprigs. Just before stew is done, cook peas as label directs. Stir in peas.

EACH SERVING: ABOUT 330 CALORIES | 32G PROTEIN | 26G CARBOHYDRATE | 11G TOTAL FAT (3G SATURATED) | 7G FIBER | 52MG CHOLESTEROL | 475MG SODIUM
☺ ♥ ✤

Coq AU RIESLING

This take on a French favorite incorporates the dryness of white wine to enhance the flavors of the herbs and vegetables. For photo, see page 42.

ACTIVE TIME: 30 MINUTES   **TOTAL TIME:** 1 HOUR   **MAKES:** 4 MAIN-DISH SERVINGS

salt and ground black pepper

1 cut-up chicken (3 to 4 pounds)

3 slices thick-cut bacon (see Tip, page 44)

4 medium leeks

2 cups baby carrots

4 cloves garlic, crushed with garlic press

1 tablespoon tomato paste

2 cups slightly dry Riesling wine

2 sprigs fresh rosemary

1 teaspoon chopped fresh thyme

2 tablespoons chopped flat-leaf parsley leaves

1 Sprinkle chicken with ¼ teaspoon salt and ⅛ teaspoon pepper.

2 In 6-quart Dutch oven, cook bacon on medium heat 6 minutes or until crisp, stirring frequently. With slotted spoon, transfer to paper towel–lined plate. Pour off and reserve drippings. Return 1 tablespoon drippings to pot; heat on medium-high. Add half of chicken; cook 7 to 10 minutes, turning once, until brown. Remove chicken to plate. Repeat with 2 teaspoons drippings and remaining chicken.

3 While chicken cooks, cut each leek lengthwise in half, then crosswise into ½-inch-wide slices. Rinse leeks thoroughly to remove any sand, repeating as necessary. Drain well.

4 To drippings remaining in Dutch oven, add leeks and carrots. Cover and cook on medium 3 minutes or until leeks begin to soften, stirring once. Add garlic and tomato paste; cook 1 minute, stirring. Add wine, rosemary, thyme, ¼ teaspoon salt, and ⅛ teaspoon pepper. Heat to boiling on high. Add chicken with any juices, placing breast pieces on top, skin side up. Reduce heat to low; cover and simmer 35 to 40 minutes or until chicken is cooked through (165°F), stirring once. Discard rosemary sprigs. Sprinkle with bacon and parsley.

EACH SERVING: ABOUT 425 CALORIES | 47G PROTEIN | 23G CARBOHYDRATE | 15G TOTAL FAT (5G SATURATED) | 3G FIBER, | 146MG CHOLESTEROL | 725MG SODIUM
♥

VALENTINE'S DAY
Red Chili

Beets and fire-roasted tomatoes color this vegetarian chili.

ACTIVE TIME: 35 MINUTES **TOTAL TIME:** 1 HOUR 30 MINUTES **MAKES:** 9 CUPS OR 6 MAIN-DISH SERVINGS

2 teaspoons ground cumin

1 teaspoon dried oregano

1/2 teaspoon chipotle chile powder

2 tablespoons vegetable oil

3 large beets (6 to 8 ounces each), trimmed, peeled, and chopped

1 jumbo red onion (1 pound), finely chopped

1 large red pepper (8 to 10 ounces), chopped

1/2 teaspoon ground black pepper

4 garlic cloves, crushed with garlic press

1 can (28 ounces) fire-roasted diced tomatoes

1 can (15 ounces) low-sodium black beans, rinsed and drained

1 can (15 ounces) low-sodium red kidney beans, rinsed and drained

1 can (15 ounces) low-sodium pinto beans, rinsed and drained

1 cup water

1 cup reduced-fat sour cream (Cabot®, Daisy®, and Breakstone's™ brands are gluten-free)

1/4 cup packed fresh cilantro leaves

1 In 7- to 8-quart Dutch oven or heavy saucepot, combine cumin, oregano, and chile powder. Cook over medium heat 1 to 2 minutes or until toasted and fragrant. Transfer to sheet of waxed paper; set aside. In same Dutch oven, heat oil over medium heat until hot. Add beets, onion, red pepper, and ¼ teaspoon black pepper. Cook 15 minutes or until vegetables are tender, stirring occasionally.

2 Add garlic and reserved spice mixture. Cook 2 minutes, stirring constantly. Add tomatoes with their juice, beans, and water. Heat to boiling over medium-high heat. Reduce heat to medium-low and simmer 30 minutes, stirring and mashing some beans occasionally. Season with remaining ¼ teaspoon black pepper. (Can be prepared to this point up to 2 days ahead; transfer to airtight container and refrigerate. Reheat before serving.) Divide among serving bowls and top with sour cream and cilantro.

EACH SERVING: ABOUT 345 CALORIES | 15G PROTEIN | 52G CARBOHYDRATE | 10G TOTAL FAT (3G SATURATED) | 15G FIBER | 13MG CHOLESTEROL | 540MG SODIUM

PORK **Posole**

Posole is made with hominy—dried white or yellow corn kernels with the hull and germ removed. It's a hearty gluten-free ingredient to add to your repertoire. Try it in meatless chili or burritos. This recipe uses canned hominy, which has already been reconstituted.

ACTIVE TIME: 45 MINUTES   **TOTAL TIME:** 2 HOURS 30 MINUTES   **MAKES:** 10 MAIN-DISH SERVINGS

2   medium red peppers

3   pounds boneless pork shoulder, well trimmed and cut into 1½-inch pieces

1   jumbo onion (1 pound), chopped

4   garlic cloves, minced

3   jalapeño chiles, seeded and minced

1   cup loosely packed fresh cilantro leaves and stems, chopped

2   teaspoons ground cumin

1½ teaspoons salt

½   teaspoon dried oregano

¼   teaspoon cayenne (ground red) pepper

1   cup water

1   can (30 ounces) hominy (posole), rinsed and drained

lime wedges, radishes, and chopped cilantro leaves, for garnish

warm gluten-free corn tortillas, for serving (optional)

1 Preheat broiler. Line broiling pan (without rack) with foil. Cut each red pepper lengthwise in half; discard stem and seeds. Arrange peppers, cut side down, in broiling pan. Place under broiler 5 to 6 inches from heat source and broil peppers until charred and blistered, 6 to 8 minutes. Wrap foil around peppers and allow to steam at room temperature until cool enough to handle, about 15 minutes. Turn oven temperature to 325°F.

2 Remove peppers from foil; peel off skin and discard. Cut peppers into 1-inch pieces.

3 In 5-quart Dutch oven, combine roasted peppers, pork, onion, garlic, jalapeños, cilantro, cumin, salt, oregano, cayenne pepper, and water; heat to boiling over high heat. Cover Dutch oven and bake until pork is very tender, about 1 hour 30 minutes.

4 Remove posole from oven; skim and discard fat. Stir in hominy; cover and bake until heated through, about 15 minutes longer. Garnish with lime wedges, radishes, and cilantro. Serve with tortillas, if desired.

EACH SERVING: ABOUT 300 CALORIES | 38G PROTEIN | 14G CARBOHYDRATE | 9G TOTAL FAT (3G SATURATED) | 3G FIBER | 83MG CHOLESTEROL | 565MG SODIUM
♥ ☺ 🍲

VIETNAMESE
Rice Noodle Soup

Although Vietnamese soup is traditionally served with thinly sliced beef, our variation uses rotisserie chicken to create a tasty twist on chicken noodle soup. The rice stick noodles—which are gluten-free— can be purchased in the Asian section of many grocery stores and in Asian markets.

ACTIVE TIME: 10 MINUTES   **TOTAL TIME:** 30 MINUTES   **MAKES:** 7½ CUPS OR 4 MAIN-DISH SERVINGS

4   ounces rice stick noodles (about ¼-inch wide)

3   green onions

3   cans (14 to 14½ ounces each) low-sodium gluten-free chicken broth (5¼ cups), such as Swanson® brand

1   cup water

1   piece (3 inches) fresh ginger, peeled and thinly sliced

¼   teaspoon Chinese five-spice powder

pinch crushed red pepper

2   cups shredded skinless rotisserie chicken meat (about 10 ounces)

fresh herbs such as basil, cilantro, and mint, chopped

lime wedges

1   Heat 3-quart saucepan of *water* to boiling over high heat. Remove from heat; add noodles, stirring to separate. Let stand 3 to 6 minutes or until noodles are tender. Drain.

2   Meanwhile, thinly slice green onions diagonally; reserve dark green tops for garnish. In 4-quart saucepan, combine light parts of green onions with broth, water, ginger, five-spice powder, and crushed red pepper; heat to boiling over high heat. Reduce heat to low; cover and simmer 10 minutes.

3   Discard ginger, if you like. Add noodles and chicken; heat to boiling over high heat.

4   Ladle soup into four bowls; serve with herbs, lime wedges to squeeze over soup, and green onion tops.

EACH SERVING: ABOUT 260 CALORIES | 24G PROTEIN | 28G CARBOHYDRATE | 5G TOTAL FAT (1G SATURATED) | 1G FIBER | 63MG CHOLESTEROL | 344MG SODIUM

Spring Vegetable Risotto
with Shrimp (page 70)

4 Stovetop Suppers

Dinner on hectic weeknights can be a challenge when you're following a gluten-free diet. You're tired, harried, short on time, and—most of all—hungry. Dietary restrictions may be the last thing you want to think about. We have the solution: everyday offerings that you can put together quickly on your stovetop with minimum fuss. Our Chicken with Smashed Potatoes, Potpie Style, and Brazilian-Style Pork Chops can be steaming on your plate in just half an hour.

But quick and easy doesn't mean you sacrifice sophistication. Tangerine Beef Stir-Fry transforms flank steak into a Chinese delight with a quick marinade of fresh tangerines plus garlic, oyster sauce, and ginger. When you find yourself longing to just coast through a drive-thru, the high nutritional quality of these recipes may make you think twice. Best of all, after sitting down to one of these satisfying meals, you may even feel less harried.

Chicken Tikka Masala 58

Chicken & Mushrooms with Brown Rice 61

Brazilian-Style Pork Chops 62

Chicken with Smashed Potatoes, Potpie Style 63

Home-Style Pad Thai 64

Tangerine Beef Stir-Fry 65

Steaks with Green Sauce 66

Steak & Tomato Sauté 69

Spring Vegetable Risotto with Shrimp 70

Caramelized Chili Shrimp Stir-Fry 71

Szechuan Chicken Pasta with Peanut Sauce 72

Spaghetti Squash "Pasta" Puttanesca 75

Chicken
TIKKA MASALA

Need a quick and flavorful meal? Put this enticing Indian chicken dish and a bowl of basmati rice on the table in just 20 minutes.

ACTIVE TIME: 10 MINUTES   **TOTAL TIME:** 20 MINUTES   **MAKES:** 4 MAIN-DISH SERVINGS

1   cup basmati rice

1   tablespoon vegetable oil

1   medium onion (6 to 8 ounces), chopped

2   teaspoons grated, peeled fresh ginger

1   garlic clove, crushed with garlic press

2   tablespoons Indian curry paste (Patak's™ brand is gluten-free)

1¼   pounds skinless, boneless chicken breast halves, cut into 1-inch chunks

¼   teaspoon salt

¼   teaspoon ground black pepper

1   cup canned crushed tomatoes

½   cup half-and-half or light cream

¼   cup loosely packed fresh cilantro leaves, chopped, plus additional for garnish

1   Prepare rice as label directs.

2   Meanwhile, in 12-inch nonstick skillet, heat oil over medium heat, 1 minute. Add onion and cook 6 minutes, stirring frequently. Add ginger, garlic, and curry paste; cook 3 minutes longer.

3   Add chicken, salt, and pepper and cook 2 minutes or until no longer pink on the outside, stirring occasionally. Add tomatoes; cover and cook 3 to 4 minutes longer or until chicken just loses its pink color throughout.

4   Uncover and stir in half-and-half and cilantro. Spoon rice into four shallow bowls; top with chicken mixture and garnish with chopped cilantro.

EACH SERVING: ABOUT 430 CALORIES | 39G PROTEIN | 42G CARBOHYDRATE | 13G TOTAL FAT (4G SATURATED) | 6G FIBER | 93MG CHOLESTEROL | 685MG SODIUM

Chicken & Mushrooms
WITH BROWN RICE

Here's a simple and wholesome weeknight meal. Everything—from the chicken to the instant brown rice and veggies—is made in a single skillet.

ACTIVE TIME: 15 MINUTES   **TOTAL TIME:** 45 MINUTES   **MAKES:** 4 MAIN-DISH SERVINGS

2	tablespoons olive oil
1¼	pounds skinless, boneless chicken thighs
1	package (10 ounces) sliced cremini mushrooms
2	medium stalks celery, thinly sliced
1	teaspoon chopped fresh thyme
1	can (14½ ounces) gluten-free chicken broth (1¾ cups), such as Swanson®
1	cup instant (10-minute) brown rice
½	cup dry white wine
¼	teaspoon salt
¼	teaspoon ground black pepper
8	baby summer squash, halved, steamed, and kept warm (optional)

1 In 12-inch skillet, heat oil over medium-high heat until hot. Add chicken and cook, covered, 5 minutes. Reduce heat to medium; turn chicken and cook, covered, 5 more minutes. Transfer to plate.

2 To skillet, add mushrooms, celery, and thyme; cook until vegetables are softened, about 5 minutes, stirring occasionally. Add broth, brown rice, wine, salt, and pepper; heat to boiling.

3 Return chicken to skillet. Reduce heat to low; cover and simmer until juices run clear when thickest part of chicken is pierced with knife and rice is cooked, about 12 minutes. Serve with steamed squash, if desired.

EACH SERVING: ABOUT 340 CALORIES | 35G PROTEIN | 21G CARBOHYDRATE | 13G TOTAL FAT (2G SATURATED) | 3G FIBER | 118MG CHOLESTEROL | 595MG SODIUM

☺ ♥

BRAZILIAN-STYLE
Pork Chops

This tasty dish is an excellent example of Brazilian cuisine: spicy with a hint of citrus and accompanied by black beans.

ACTIVE TIME: 15 MINUTES   **TOTAL TIME:** 30 MINUTES   **MAKES:** 4 MAIN-DISH SERVINGS

4	boneless pork loin chops, 3/4-inch thick (5 ounces each), trimmed
1/2	teaspoon ground cumin
1/2	teaspoon ground coriander
1/4	teaspoon dried thyme
1/8	teaspoon ground allspice
1/2	teaspoon salt
1	teaspoon olive oil
1	onion, chopped
3	garlic cloves, crushed with garlic press
1	can (15 to 19 ounces) black beans, rinsed and drained
1/2	cup gluten-free chicken broth, such as Swanson®
1	tablespoon fresh lime juice
1/4	teaspoon ground black pepper
1/4	cup packed fresh cilantro leaves, chopped
fresh orange wedges (optional)	

1 Pat pork chops dry with paper towels. In cup, mix cumin, coriander, thyme, allspice, and 1/4 teaspoon salt. Rub pork chops with spice mixture.

2 Heat nonstick 12-inch skillet over medium heat until hot. Add pork chops and cook until lightly browned outside and still slightly pink inside, about 4 minutes per side. Transfer pork to platter; keep warm.

3 In same skillet, heat oil over medium heat. Add onion and cook, stirring frequently, until golden, about 5 minutes. Add garlic and cook, stirring, 1 minute longer. Add beans, broth, lime juice, pepper, and remaining 1/4 teaspoon salt; heat through.

4 To serve, spoon bean mixture over pork; sprinkle with cilantro. Serve with orange wedges, if you like.

EACH SERVING: ABOUT 340 CALORIES | 42G PROTEIN | 25G CARBOHYDRATE | 11G TOTAL FAT (3G SATURATED) | 10G FIBER | 76MG CHOLESTEROL | 760MG SODIUM

Chicken with Smashed Potatoes, POTPIE STYLE

Newsflash, potpie lovers: You can tuck into this comforting rendition, which features potpie filling atop creamy mashed potatoes. Unlike the classic dish, it's 100-percent gluten-free.

ACTIVE TIME: 10 MINUTES   TOTAL TIME: 30 MINUTES   MAKES: 4 MAIN-DISH SERVINGS

1½ pounds baby red potatoes, cut in half

1 tablespoon vegetable oil

4 medium skinless, boneless chicken breast halves (1¼ pounds)

½ teaspoon salt

¼ teaspoon ground black pepper

2 medium carrots, cut into 2" by ¼" matchstick strips (1½ cups)

1 cup gluten-free chicken broth, such as Swanson®

¼ cup heavy or whipping cream

½ teaspoon dried tarragon, crumbled

1 cup tiny frozen peas, thawed

1 tablespoon butter

fresh tarragon sprigs, for garnish (optional)

1 In 5-quart Dutch oven, combine potatoes and enough *water* to cover; heat to boiling over high heat. Reduce heat to medium; cover and simmer until potatoes are fork-tender, about 12 minutes.

2 Meanwhile, in nonstick 12-inch skillet, heat oil over medium heat until hot. Add chicken and sprinkle with ¼ teaspoon salt and ⅛ teaspoon pepper; cook 6 minutes. Turn chicken over, cover, and cook until juices run clear when thickest part of chicken is pierced with knife, about 8 minutes longer. Transfer chicken to plate; keep warm.

3 To same skillet, add carrots, broth, cream, and dried tarragon; cover and cook over medium-high heat until carrots are tender, about 5 minutes. Remove skillet from heat and stir in peas.

4 Drain potatoes and return to pot. Coarsely mash potatoes with butter and remaining ¼ teaspoon salt and ⅛ teaspoon pepper.

5 To serve, spoon potatoes onto large platter; top with chicken and spoon vegetable mixture over all. Garnish with tarragon sprigs, if desired.

EACH SERVING: ABOUT 455 CALORIES | 39G PROTEIN | 43G CARBOHYDRATE | 14G TOTAL FAT (4G SATURATED) | 5G FIBER | 110MG CHOLESTEROL | 637MG SODIUM

HOME-STYLE
Pad Thai

Enjoy this takeout classic at home—gluten-free. Our recipe includes both tofu and shrimp, though you can use one or the other, if you prefer.

ACTIVE TIME: 20 MINUTES   **TOTAL TIME:** 30 MINUTES   **MAKES:** 4 MAIN-DISH SERVINGS

8   ounces thin rice noodles (about ⅛-inch wide)

3 to 4 limes

4   ounces firm tofu, cut into ½-inch cubes (about ¾ cup)

3   tablespoons reduced-sodium fish sauce (A Taste of Thai® and Chun's™ brand make gluten-free versions)

2   tablespoons sugar

8   ounces medium shrimp, shelled and deveined

2   garlic cloves, finely chopped

¼   teaspoon cayenne (ground red) pepper

2   large eggs, lightly beaten

2   cups packed thinly sliced Napa cabbage (about 5 ounces)

1   cup (3 ounces) fresh bean sprouts

½   cup loosely packed fresh cilantro leaves, chopped

¼   cup unsalted roasted peanuts, coarsely chopped

2   teaspoons vegetable oil

2   green onions, thinly sliced

1   Soak rice noodles in large bowl containing enough *hot tap water* to cover. Let stand 20 minutes; drain.

2   Meanwhile, squeeze 2 or 3 limes to make ¼ cup juice; set aside. Cut remaining lime into wedges; set aside. Place tofu between several layers of paper towels and press lightly to drain.

3   In small bowl, combine fish sauce, lime juice, and sugar. Position the following items in individual bowls near stovetop: tofu, shrimp, garlic, cayenne, eggs, cabbage, bean sprouts, cilantro, and peanuts.

4   In 12-inch skillet, heat oil over medium-high heat until hot. Add tofu and cook 5 minutes or until golden, stirring occasionally. Return tofu to bowl.

5   In same skillet, cook shrimp, garlic, and cayenne pepper over medium-high heat 2 to 3 minutes, stirring until shrimp are no longer pink. Stir in eggs and cook about 30 seconds or until eggs start to set.

6   Add drained noodles, tofu, sliced cabbage, and fish sauce mixture to skillet. Using tongs or two forks, toss to combine, and cook 2 minutes longer. Remove skillet from heat. Add bean sprouts, cilantro, peanuts, and green onions; toss to mix well. Serve with lime wedges and additional fish sauce.

EACH SERVING: ABOUT 495 CALORIES | 20G PROTEIN | 64G CARBOHYDRATE | 19G TOTAL FAT (2G SATURATED) | 3G FIBER | 106MG CHOLESTEROL | 840MG SODIUM

TANGERINE BEEF **Stir-Fry**

Hassle-free flank steak, sliced into quick-sizzling strips, is the shortcut in this citrus-spiked dish. Marinating the meat in a garlicky ginger-tangerine sauce amps up the Chinese-takeout taste. Serve over hot fluffy white rice or substitute brown rice for more fiber, if you like.

ACTIVE TIME: 30 MINUTES   **TOTAL TIME:** 35 MINUTES   **MAKES:** 4 MAIN-DISH SERVINGS

1   cup long-grain white rice

2   tangerines

2   garlic cloves, crushed with garlic press

1   tablespoon oyster sauce, such as Lee Kum Kee's™ Panda Breen Green Label Oyster Flavored Sauce

1   teaspoon honey

1/2   teaspoon ground ginger

1/4   teaspoon Chinese five-spice powder

3/8   teaspoon salt

1/4   teaspoon ground black pepper

1   pound beef flank steak, cut in half lengthwise and thinly sliced across grain

2   tablespoons vegetable oil

12   ounces cremini mushrooms, thinly sliced

12   ounces snow peas

4   green onions, cut into 1-inch pieces

1   Prepare rice as label directs. Meanwhile, with vegetable peeler, remove peel from 1 tangerine in strips. From both tangerines, squeeze 1/2 cup juice. To large resealable bag, add peel, juice, half of garlic, oyster sauce, honey, ginger, five-spice powder, 1/4 teaspoon salt, pepper, and beef. Seal bag and let stand 10 minutes.

2   Meanwhile, in 12-inch skillet, heat 1 tablespoon oil over medium-high heat until hot. Add mushrooms, remaining garlic, and remaining 1/8 teaspoon salt. Cook 3 to 4 minutes or until mushrooms are tender, stirring occasionally. Add snow peas and cook 3 minutes or until snow peas are tender-crisp, stirring occasionally. Transfer to large plate.

3   To same skillet, add remaining oil and heat over medium-high heat until hot. Add beef and marinade; cook 4 minutes or until beef is no longer pink, stirring occasionally. Add mushroom mixture and green onions, tossing to combine. Cook 2 minutes or until green onions have wilted, stirring occasionally. Serve with rice.

EACH SERVING: ABOUT 505 CALORIES | 33G PROTEIN | 58G CARBOHYDRATE | 16G TOTAL FAT (4G SATURATED) | 4G FIBER | 40MG CHOLESTEROL | 415MG SODIUM ♥

Steaks WITH GREEN SAUCE

Pairing steak with a sauce of parsley and cornichon pickles adds a briny contrast to the meat. A grill pan brings the ease of grilling indoors any time of the year.

ACTIVE TIME: 15 MINUTES   TOTAL TIME: 20 MINUTES   MAKES: 4 MAIN-DISH SERVINGS

2   boneless top loin steaks (about ¾ pound each)

cooking spray

¼   teaspoon salt

¼   teaspoon ground black pepper

2   cups chopped parsley

⅓   cup chopped cornichons plus 3 tablespoons cornichon juice

¼   cup extra-virgin olive oil

1   tablespoon water

1 Lightly spray steaks with nonstick cooking spray; season with salt and pepper.

2 Heat grill pan on medium-high until hot. Cook steaks 8 to 10 minutes or until desired doneness (140°F for medium-rare), turning over once. Transfer to cutting board and let steaks rest.

3 Meanwhile, in a small bowl, whisk parsley, cornichons and their juice, olive oil, and water. Serve steaks with sauce.

....

EACH SERVING: ABOUT 385 CALORIES | 28G PROTEIN | 7G CARBOHYDRATE | 28G TOTAL FAT (7G SATURATED) | 1G FIBER | 83MG CHOLESTEROL | 468MG SODIUM ✅

STEAK & TOMATO
Sauté

Lean sirloin gets the steakhouse treatment with savory mushrooms, onions, and red wine. A bed of arugula packs in peppery flavor— and disease-fighting antioxidants.

ACTIVE TIME: 20 MINUTES   **TOTAL TIME:** 30 MINUTES   **MAKES:** 4 MAIN-DISH SERVINGS

2   tablespoons vegetable oil

1¼ pounds top sirloin beef steak, trimmed and thinly sliced into 2-inch-long pieces

salt and ground black pepper

1   medium onion, thinly sliced

⅓   cup water

1   container (10 ounces) sliced mushrooms

1   pint grape tomatoes

⅔   cup dry red wine

2   cloves garlic, crushed with garlic press

6   cups arugula (about 4 ounces)

1 In 12-inch skillet, heat oil on medium-high until hot, but not smoking. Sprinkle beef with ⅛ teaspoon salt and ¼ teaspoon pepper. Add beef to skillet; cook 2 minutes or until browned, stirring occasionally.

2 With slotted spoon, transfer beef to medium plate. To same skillet, add onion and water. Cook 2 minutes, scraping up browned bits. Add mushrooms, tomatoes, and ¼ teaspoon salt. Cook 3 to 4 minutes or until onion softens.

3 To skillet, add red wine and garlic. Cover and cook 5 to 7 minutes or until tomatoes begin to burst, stirring occasionally. Return beef to skillet along with any accumulated juices. Cook 1 minute or until beef is heated through (145°F).

4 To serve, divide arugula among serving plates. Top with beef mixture.

EACH SERVING: ABOUT 310 CALORIES | 36G PROTEIN | 12G CARBOHYDRATE | 13G TOTAL FAT (3G SATURATED) | 3G FIBER | 85MG CHOLESTEROL | 320MG SODIUM

Spring Vegetable Risotto
WITH SHRIMP

The perfect company fare, this medley of asparagus, peas, carrots, and shrimp is as colorful as it is delicious. Arborio rice, a creamy short-grained rice, is the classic choice for risotto. For photo, see page 56.

ACTIVE TIME: 10 MINUTES   **TOTAL TIME:** 35 MINUTES   **MAKES:** 10 CUPS OR 6 MAIN-DISH SERVINGS

1   carton (32 ounces) gluten-free chicken broth, such as Swanson®

1¼ cups water

½ cup dry white wine

8   ounces asparagus, cut into 1-inch pieces

1   tablespoon olive oil

1   small onion (4 to 6 ounces), finely chopped

1   carrot, peeled and finely chopped

2   cups Arborio or carnaroli rice

1   pound shelled and deveined large shrimp

1   cup frozen peas

2   tablespoons fresh lemon juice

1   tablespoon chopped fresh parsley or basil leaves

¼ teaspoon salt

¼ teaspoon ground black pepper

1 In 2-quart saucepan, heat broth, water, and wine to boiling over high heat. When boiling, add asparagus and cook 2 minutes. With slotted spoon, remove asparagus to small bowl; set aside.

2 Meanwhile, in microwave-safe 4-quart bowl or casserole dish, combine oil, onion, and carrot. Cook, uncovered, in microwave on high 3 minutes or until vegetables begin to soften. Add rice and stir to coat with oil; cook, uncovered, on high 1 minute.

3 Stir hot broth mixture into rice mixture. Cover bowl with vented plastic wrap and microwave on medium 15 minutes or until most of liquid is absorbed and rice is tender but still firm, stirring halfway through cooking.

4 Add shrimp, frozen peas, and cooked asparagus; cover and cook in microwave on high 3 to 4 minutes longer or just until shrimp lose their pink color throughout. Do not overcook; mixture will look loose and soupy but will thicken to the proper creamy consistency after cooking.

5 Stir in lemon juice, parsley, salt, and pepper.

EACH SERVING: ABOUT 425 CALORIES | 24G PROTEIN | 67G CARBOHYDRATE | 4G TOTAL FAT (1G SATURATED) | 3G FIBER | 115MG CHOLESTEROL | 545MG SODIUM
♥ ☺

CARAMELIZED CHILI
Shrimp Stir-Fry

Thanks to a trio of convenient instant ingredients—preshelled shrimp, rice vermicelli, and bagged broccoli, each of which cooks in three minutes—this streamlined seafood stir-fry is ideal for time-is-tight nights. Red pepper flakes add a hit of heat.

ACTIVE TIME: 15 MINUTES   **TOTAL TIME:** 25 MINUTES   **MAKES:** 4 MAIN-DISH SERVINGS

- 6 ounces rice stick noodles (vermicelli)
- 1 pound broccoli florets
- 1 green onion, finely chopped
- ¼ teaspoon salt
- 3 tablespoons sugar
- 1 tablespoon water
- 1 tablespoon vegetable oil
- 3 garlic cloves, very thinly sliced
- ¼ teaspoon crushed red pepper
- 1 tablespoon lower-sodium fish sauce (A Taste of Thai® and Chun's™ make gluten-free versions)
- 1 pound shrimp (16 to 20 count), peeled and deveined
- ¼ cup packed fresh cilantro leaves
- ¼ teaspoon ground black pepper

1 In heavy 12-inch skillet, heat *1 inch water* to boiling over high heat. Add noodles and cook 1 to 2 minutes or until just tender. With tongs, transfer noodles to colander. Rinse under cold water and drain. Leave water-filled skillet on heat.

2 When water in skillet returns to boiling, add broccoli. Cook 3 minutes or until tender-crisp; drain and transfer to large bowl. Toss with green onion and salt. Wipe skillet dry.

3 In same skillet, cook sugar and water over medium-high heat (stirring just until sugar dissolves), 3 to 4 minutes or until mixture turns dark amber. Stir in oil, garlic, and crushed red pepper. Cook 10 seconds, then stir in fish sauce and shrimp.

4 Cook, stirring often, 2 to 3 minutes or until shrimp just turn opaque throughout. Remove from heat and stir in cilantro and black pepper.

5 Divide noodles and broccoli among serving plates. Spoon shrimp with sauce on top of noodles.

EACH SERVING: ABOUT 340 CALORIES | 22G PROTEIN | 53G CARBOHYDRATE | 5G TOTAL FAT (1G SATURATED) | 4G FIBER | 168MG CHOLESTEROL | 600MG SODIUM

Szechuan Chicken Pasta
WITH PEANUT SAUCE

This ground chicken and mixed veggie noodle dish features
a yummy Asian-style peanut sauce.

ACTIVE TIME: 10 MINUTES   TOTAL TIME: 25 MINUTES   MAKES: 6 MAIN-DISH SERVINGS

1   pound gluten-free spaghetti

1   teaspoon vegetable oil

2   bunches green onions, cut into 1/2-inch pieces

1   pound ground chicken or turkey breast meat

2   tablespoons grated, peeled fresh ginger

3   garlic cloves, crushed with garlic press

1   tablespoon gluten-free cornstarch (see Tip, page 17)

3   tablespoons reduced-sodium tamari, such as San-J™

1/4   cup orange juice

1   bag (12 to 16 ounces) shredded broccoli, cauliflower, carrot, and cabbage blend

1   can (14 1/2 ounces) gluten-free chicken broth (1 3/4 cups), such as Swanson®

1/4   cup natural creamy peanut butter (see Tip, page 116)

hot pepper sauce (optional)

1 Cook spaghetti as label directs.

2 Meanwhile, in 12-inch skillet, heat oil over high heat. Add green onions and cook, stirring, 1 to 2 minutes or until wilted; transfer to bowl.

3 In same skillet over high heat, cook chicken, ginger, and garlic 3 minutes or until chicken is no longer pink, stirring to break up chicken.

4 In a 2-cup glass measuring cup, whisk together cornstarch, tamari, and orange juice until no lumps remain. Add to skillet along with vegetable blend, broth, peanut butter, and green onions; heat to boiling. Reduce heat to medium and cook 6 to 8 minutes or until vegetables are tender-crisp and sauce thickens slightly, stirring.

5 Drain spaghetti; return to saucepot. Add chicken mixture and toss to combine. Serve with hot pepper sauce, if you like.

EACH SERVING: ABOUT 475 CALORIES | 34G PROTEIN | 70G CARBOHYDRATE | 9G TOTAL FAT (1G SATURATED) | 10G FIBER | 44MG CHOLESTEROL | 580MG SODIUM

SPAGHETTI SQUASH
"Pasta" Puttanesca

This vegetable dish, disguised as a pasta, is a fresh and flavorful gluten-free take on an Italian classic.

ACTIVE TIME: 20 MINUTES   **TOTAL TIME:** 30 MINUTES   **MAKES:** 4 MAIN-DISH SERVINGS

1   large spaghetti squash (4 to 4½ pounds)

1   pint grape or cherry tomatoes, cut into quarters

½   cup loosely packed fresh basil leaves, thinly sliced, plus additional leaves for garnish

2   cans (5 ounces each) white or light tuna in water, drained and flaked

¼   cup pitted Kalamata olives, chopped

1   tablespoon drained capers, coarsely chopped

1   tablespoon olive oil

2   teaspoons red wine vinegar

½   teaspoon salt

¼   teaspoon ground black pepper

freshly grated Parmesan cheese

1   Place squash in 9-inch glass pie plate and pierce six times with sharp knife. Microwave on high 5 to 6 minutes per pound, about 20 minutes total, or until squash is tender when pierced with knife. Cool 10 minutes for easier handling.

2   Meanwhile, in medium bowl, mix tomatoes, basil, tuna, olives, capers, oil, vinegar, ¼ teaspoon salt, and ⅛ teaspoon pepper until combined.

3   Cut squash lengthwise in half; remove and discard seeds. With fork, scrape flesh to separate into strands and place in large bowl; discard shell. Drain squash if necessary. Add remaining ¼ teaspoon salt and ⅛ teaspoon pepper; toss to combine.

4   Divide squash among 4 dinner bowls. To serve, top with tomato mixture; garnish with basil leaves and Parmesan.

EACH SERVING: ABOUT 245 CALORIES | 17G PROTEIN | 28G CARBOHYDRATE | 8G TOTAL FAT (2G SATURATED) | 5G FIBER | 24MG CHOLESTEROL | 705MG SODIUM

Jerk Pork Chops with
Grilled Pineapple (page 83)

5 Grilled Favorites

You may give up a lot of foods on a gluten-free diet, but you can be thankful that meat isn't one of them. In fact, just about anything you can throw on the searing rack of a grill is deliciously fair game for gluten-free eating. Vegetables taste richer after taking on the charred flavor of flame roasting, in part because fire concentrates their sugars, making them both smoky and sweet—check out our Mexican Veggie Stacks to see what we mean.

The flavors of summer will come through loud and clear in these recipes, many of which give protein and vegetables space on the grill at the same time. You'll find a number of intriguing approaches to classic grill-worthy meats and seafood, like the alluring flavor combination in Coffee-Spice Chicken with Fruit-Basil Salsa. Burgers take on a new character with ground turkey spiced up with Jamaican jerk seasoning in our Jerk Turkey Burgers.

Sweet & Tangy Barbecued Chicken 78

Coffee-Spice Chicken with Fruit-Basil Salsa 80

Jerk Turkey Burgers 82

Jerk Pork Chops with Grilled Pineapple 83

Sausage-Pepper Kabobs 85

Korean Steak in Lettuce Cups 87

Fire-Grilled Steak 88

Miso-Glazed Salmon with Edamame Salad 90

Mexican Veggie Stacks 92

Ratatouille on the Grill 93

SWEET & TANGY
Barbecued Chicken

It wouldn't be an American summer get-together without barbecued chicken. Our crowd-pleasing recipe precooks the chicken in the oven—so you can make it a day ahead (and not fret about burnt or undercooked chicken). Then, when you're ready to dine, just warm up the chicken on the grill and brush on our luscious gluten-free sauce.

ACTIVE TIME: 25 MINUTES   **TOTAL TIME:** 2 HOURS   **MAKES:** 12 MAIN-DISH SERVINGS

3   chickens (4 pounds each), quartered with skin removed

2½ teaspoons salt

2   lemons, cut into wedges

1   large onion (12 ounces), cut into wedges

2   cans (14½ ounces each) no-salt-added tomatoes

¼   cup balsamic vinegar

4   teaspoons honey

4   teaspoons spicy brown mustard (Heinz® and French's® are gluten-free)

2   garlic cloves, crushed with garlic press

1   teaspoon smoked paprika

2   Gala apples, chopped

1 Preheat oven to 425°F. Arrange chicken quarters in large roasting pan (17" by 11½"), overlapping pieces if necessary. Sprinkle chicken with 1½ teaspoons salt; top with lemon and onion wedges. Cover roasting pan tightly with heavy-duty foil. Oven-steam chicken until juices run clear when thickest part of chicken is pierced with tip of knife, about 1 hour 15 minutes, turning chicken over halfway through baking time to ensure even cooking. Discard lemons and onion. Refrigerate broth for another use. Transfer chicken to large platter; cover and refrigerate until ready to grill.

2 Meanwhile, prepare barbecue sauce: In 2-quart saucepan, combine tomatoes with their juice, vinegar, honey, mustard, garlic, paprika, 1 teaspoon salt, and apples. Bring to a boil over high heat; reduce heat to medium and simmer 30 minutes. Puree in blender until smooth. (Makes 4 cups.)

3 Transfer sauce to bowl or, if not using right away, transfer to airtight container. (Sauce will keep, refrigerated, for up to 2 weeks.)

4 Prepare outdoor grill for covered direct grilling over medium heat. Place chicken on hot grill rack over medium heat; cover grill and cook 10 minutes, turning chicken over once. Reserve 3 cups barbecue sauce to serve with grilled chicken. Cook chicken 5 to 10 minutes longer, turning over occasionally and frequently brushing with remaining barbecue sauce until chicken is heated through and sauce is browned. Heat reserved barbecue sauce to serve with chicken.

EACH SERVING: ABOUT 315 CALORIES | 44G PROTEIN | 6G CARBOHYDRATE | 12G TOTAL FAT (3G SATURATED) | 1G FIBER | 135MG CHOLESTEROL | 540MG SODIUM
☺ ♥ 🧺

Coffee-Spice Chicken
WITH FRUIT-BASIL SALSA

A jerk-style seasoning of Jamaican allspice and java gives this Caribbean chicken its caffeinated kick. Balancing the heat: a cooling summer salsa of fresh nectarine and juicy watermelon.

ACTIVE TIME: 30 MINUTES   **TOTAL TIME:** 40 MINUTES   **MAKES:** 8 MAIN-DISH SERVINGS

3   cups seedless watermelon cubes, cut into ½-inch chunks (from 4-pound piece of watermelon)

1   large ripe nectarine, pitted and cut into ½-inch chunks

3   tablespoons finely chopped red onion

1   tablespoon fresh lemon juice

2   tablespoons instant unflavored coffee

1   tablespoon grated, peeled fresh ginger

1   tablespoon olive oil

1¼ teaspoons ground allspice

¾   teaspoon salt

8   skinless, boneless chicken breast halves (3 pounds)

½   cup packed fresh basil leaves, coarsely chopped

1 In medium bowl, combine watermelon, nectarine, red onion, and lemon juice. Cover and refrigerate while preparing chicken. (Makes 4 cups.)

2 Prepare outdoor grill for covered direct grilling over medium heat.

3 In large bowl, with spoon or fingers, press coffee to pulverize. Add ginger, oil, allspice, and ½ teaspoon salt; stir to combine. Add chicken and toss to evenly coat with spice mixture (you may need to pat mixture onto chicken with your fingers).

4 Place chicken breasts on hot grill grate. Cover and cook 8 to 10 minutes or until juices run clear when thickest part of chicken is pierced with tip of knife, turning over once. Transfer chicken to cutting board and let rest 5 minutes. Meanwhile, stir basil and remaining ¼ teaspoon salt into salsa. Slice chicken crosswise and serve with salsa.

EACH SERVING: ABOUT 235 CALORIES | 40G PROTEIN | 8G CARBOHYDRATE | 4G TOTAL FAT (1G SATURATED) | 1G FIBER | 99MG CHOLESTEROL | 310MG SODIUM ☺ ♥

JERK
Turkey Burgers

When ground turkey is spiced up with Jamaican jerk seasoning and fresh thyme, burger night takes on a juicy and flavorful edge. Gluten-free hamburger buns are available, but you could also choose to serve these spicy patties on the more widely available gluten-free English muffins or wrapped up in gluten-free tortillas.

ACTIVE TIME: 10 MINUTES   **TOTAL TIME:** 25 MINUTES   **MAKES:** 4 BURGERS

⅓ cup reduced-fat mayonnaise (Hellman's® Lite Mayonnaise is gluten-free)

2 teaspoons chopped fresh thyme

¼ teaspoon freshly grated orange peel

1¼ pounds ground turkey or chicken

2 green onions, chopped

1 small jalapeño chile with seeds, chopped

¼ teaspoon salt

4 teaspoons Jamaican jerk seasoning

nonstick cooking spray

4 gluten-free multigrain hamburger buns, split and toasted

lettuce leaves

1 Prepare outdoor grill for direct grilling over medium heat.

2 In small bowl, stir mayonnaise, thyme, and orange peel until well blended. Set sauce aside. (Makes about ⅓ cup.)

3 In medium bowl, combine turkey, green onions, jalapeño, and salt just until blended. Shape mixture into four ¾-inch-thick burgers. On a sheet of waxed paper, pat jerk seasoning onto both sides of burgers. Lightly spray both sides of burgers with cooking spray.

4 Place burgers on hot grill rack; cook 12 to 14 minutes or until juices run clear when center of burger is pierced with tip of knife, turning over once. (An instant-read meat thermometer inserted horizontally into center should register 170°F.)

5 Serve burgers on buns with lettuce and sauce.

· ·

EACH SERVING: ABOUT 415 CALORIES | 30G PROTEIN | 34G CARBOHYDRATE | 19G TOTAL FAT (4G SATURATED) | 2G FIBER | 94MG CHOLESTEROL | 890MG SODIUM

Jerk Pork Chops
WITH GRILLED PINEAPPLE

Expand your pork chop horizons with a unique dish paired with grilled fresh pineapple. For photo, see page 76.

ACTIVE TIME: 20 MINUTES   **TOTAL TIME:** 20 MINUTES   **MAKES:** 4 MAIN-DISH SERVINGS

1   tablespoon olive oil

1   tablespoon packed light brown sugar

1   tablespoon jerk seasoning

1   tablespoon grated lime peel

2   cloves garlic, crushed with garlic press

1/2   teaspoon cayenne (ground red) pepper

4   bone-in pork loin chops (about 1 pound each)

2   sweet potatoes, sliced into 1 1/2-inch pieces

1   pineapple, sliced into 1/2-inch pieces

cooking spray

4   green onions, chopped

lime wedges, for serving

1 Prepare grill for direct grilling over medium-high heat.

2 In a small bowl, stir together olive oil, brown sugar, jerk seasoning, grated lime peel, garlic, and cayenne pepper. Rub spice mixture onto 4 pork chops. Coat the sweet potato and pineapple slices with cooking spray.

3 Grill pork, pineapple, and sweet potatoes for 10 minutes or until tender and pork is cooked (145°F), turning over once. Transfer to cutting board; cut potatoes and pineapple into wedges.

4 Divide pork chops, sweet potatoes, and pineapple among 4 plates. Sprinkle with green onions and serve with lime wedges.

EACH SERVING: ABOUT 440 CALORIES | 28G PROTEIN | 51G CARBOHYDRATE | 15G TOTAL FAT (4G SATURATED) | 4G FIBER | 81MG CHOLESTEROL | 310MG SODIUM

SAUSAGE-PEPPER
Kabobs

Grilled smoked sausage and fresh vegetables make a great light summer or holiday meal. To save time, these kabobs can be prepped a day before serving, wrapped, and refrigerated.

TOTAL TIME: 35 MINUTES   **MAKES:** 12 MAIN-DISH SERVINGS

12	metal or bamboo skewers
¼	cup olive oil
2	cloves garlic, crushed with garlic press
½	teaspoon dried oregano
⅛	teaspoon salt
⅛	teaspoon ground black pepper
2	large onions
2	medium green peppers
3	medium red peppers
2	pounds fully-cooked kielbasa (smoked Polish sausage)

1 If using bamboo skewers, soak skewers in cold water at least 30 minutes to prevent burning. Prepare outdoor grill for covered direct grilling over medium heat.

2 In small bowl, combine oil, garlic, oregano, salt, and pepper. Let stand while you cut onions, peppers, and sausages into 1-inch chunks.

3 Thread peppers, two at a time and alternating with onion and sausage, onto skewers. Brush skewers with oil mixture.

4 Place on hot grill grate; cover and cook 10 to 12 minutes or until browned, turning occasionally. Place on platter to serve.

EACH SERVING: ABOUT 235 CALORIES | 11G PROTEIN | 8G CARBOHYDRATE | 18G TOTAL FAT (5G SATURATED) | 2G FIBER | 53MG CHOLESTEROL | 934MG SODIUM

Korean Steak
IN LETTUCE CUPS

No bread required for these wraps. Set out bowls of crisp romaine lettuce, rice, green onions, and sesame seeds and let each person assemble his or her own package.

ACTIVE TIME: 40 MINUTES **TOTAL TIME:** 55 MINUTES PLUS MARINATING AND STANDING
MAKES: 6 MAIN-DISH SERVINGS

½ cup reduced-sodium tamari, such as San-J™

2 tablespoons sugar

2 tablespoons minced, peeled fresh ginger

2 tablespoons seasoned rice vinegar

1 tablespoon Asian sesame oil

¼ teaspoon cayenne (ground red) pepper

3 garlic cloves, crushed with garlic press

1 beef top round or sirloin steak, 1-inch thick (1½ pounds)

1 cup regular long-grain rice

¼ cup water

3 green onions, thinly sliced

1 tablespoon sesame seeds, toasted

1 head romaine lettuce, separated into leaves

1 In large zip-tight plastic bag, combine tamari, sugar, ginger, vinegar, sesame oil, cayenne pepper, and garlic; add steak, turning to coat. Seal bag, pressing out air. Place on plate; refrigerate 1 to 4 hours, turning once.

2 Prepare outdoor grill for direct grilling over medium heat. Just before grilling steak, prepare rice according to package directions; keep warm.

3 Remove steak from bag; reserve marinade. Place steak on hot grill rack over medium heat and grill, turning once, 14 to 15 minutes for medium-rare or until desired doneness. Transfer steak to cutting board; let stand 10 minutes to allow juices to set for easier slicing.

4 In 1-quart saucepan, heat reserved marinade and water to boiling over high heat; boil 2 minutes.

5 To serve, thinly slice steak. Let each person place steak, rice, green onions, and sesame seeds on a lettuce leaf, then drizzle with cooked marinade. Fold sides of lettuce leaf over filling to form a packet to eat like a sandwich.

EACH SERVING: ABOUT 370 CALORIES | 30G PROTEIN | 35G CARBOHYDRATE | 11G TOTAL FAT (3G SATURATED) | 3G FIBER | 69MG CHOLESTEROL | 960MG SODIUM
☺ ♥

FIRE-GRILLED
Steak

Grilled steak and vegetables get big flavor from heart-healthy olive oil, tangy vinegar, fresh herbs, and capers.

TOTAL TIME: 30 MINUTES   **MAKES:** 4 MAIN-DISH SERVINGS

1   beef flank steak (1½ pounds)

salt and ground black pepper

5   teaspoons extra-virgin olive oil

2   medium fennel bulbs, cored and sliced

1   large red onion, thinly sliced

½   cup fresh mint leaves

½   cup fresh flat-leaf parsley leaves

3   tablespoons red wine vinegar

2   tablespoons capers

1   small clove garlic, crushed with garlic press

1   tablespoon water

1 Prepare outdoor grill for covered direct grilling over medium heat. Sprinkle steak with ¼ teaspoon each salt and pepper to season both sides. Use 2 teaspoons oil to brush both sides of fennel and onion slices; sprinkle with ⅛ teaspoon salt.

2 Grill steak, covered, 8 to 10 minutes for medium-rare or until desired doneness, turning over once. Grill onion alongside steak, 7 to 9 minutes or until tender. Transfer steak to cutting board; let rest 10 minutes. Transfer onion to bowl.

3 Meanwhile, finely chop mint and parsley; place in medium bowl with vinegar, capers, garlic, water, and remaining 3 teaspoons oil. Stir to blend.

4 Place fennel on grill. Cover; cook 3 to 4 minutes or until browned, turning over once. Toss with onion.

5 Thinly slice steak. Serve with fennel, onion, and vinaigrette.

....

EACH SERVING: ABOUT 329 CALORIES | 32G PROTEIN | 14G CARBOHYDRATE | 16G TOTAL FAT (5G SATURATED) | 6G FIBER | 86MG CHOLESTEROL | 446MG SODIUM

♥ ♥ ☺

Miso-Glazed Salmon
WITH EDAMAME SALAD

Spread a mixture of miso, ginger, and cayenne pepper on a large salmon fillet. Enjoy with our healthy soybean salad for a Japanese-inspired meal.

ACTIVE TIME: 30 MINUTES   **TOTAL TIME:** 40 MINUTES   **MAKES:** 4 MAIN-DISH SERVINGS

EDAMAME SALAD

- 1   bag (16 ounces) frozen shelled edamame (green soybeans)
- ¼   cup seasoned rice vinegar
- 1   tablespoon vegetable oil
- 1   teaspoon sugar
- ¾   teaspoon salt
- ⅛   teaspoon ground black pepper
- 1   bunch radishes (8 ounces), cut in half and thinly sliced
- 1   cup loosely packed fresh cilantro leaves, chopped

MISO-GLAZED SALMON

- 2   tablespoons white miso (see Tip; Eden® brand is gluten-free)
- 1   green onion, minced
- 1   tablespoon grated, peeled fresh ginger
- 1   teaspoon brown sugar
- ⅛   teaspoon cayenne (ground red) pepper
- 1   salmon fillet with skin on (1½ pounds)

1 **Prepare Edamame Salad:** Cook edamame as label directs. Drain and rinse with cold running water to stop cooking; drain again. In medium bowl, whisk vinegar, oil, sugar, salt, and pepper until blended. Add edamame, radishes, and cilantro; toss to coat. (Makes about 4 cups.)

2 Prepare outdoor grill for direct grilling over medium-low heat.

3 **Prepare Miso-Glazed Salmon:** With tweezers, remove any pinbones from salmon. In small bowl, mix miso, green onion, ginger, brown sugar, and cayenne pepper. Rub miso mixture on flesh side of salmon.

4 Place salmon, skin side down, on hot grill rack and grill until just opaque throughout, 10 to 12 minutes, turning once. Serve with Edamame Salad.

> **TIP**
>
> Miso, a Japanese culinary mainstay, is made from fermented soybeans. However, whether it's gluten-free or not depends on the *koji* (yeast-like fermenting agent) that's used. Look for those that use rice- or soybean-based *koji* (typically true of white misos); avoid barley-based versions.

EACH SERVING (SALMON WITH 1 CUP SALAD): ABOUT 500 CALORIES | 45G PROTEIN | 26G CARBOHYDRATE | 24G TOTAL FAT (3G SATURATED) | 6G FIBER | 80MG CHOLESTEROL | 1,470MG SODIUM ♥

MEXICAN **Veggie Stacks**

Warm a foil packet of corn tortillas on the grill to make this a full meal.

ACTIVE TIME: 25 MINUTES   TOTAL TIME: 45 MINUTES   MAKES: 4 MAIN-DISH SERVINGS

1   tablespoon regular chili powder

3   tablespoons olive oil

¾   teaspoon salt

⅛   cup chopped fresh cilantro

2   tablespoons fresh lime juice

1   large poblano chile (6 ounces)

2   ears corn, husks and silks removed

1   large red onion (1 pound), cut crosswise into slices

1   medium zucchini (10 ounces), cut diagonally into ½-inch-thick slices

2   large ripe tomatoes (10 to 12 ounces each), cut horizontally in half

4   ounces jalapeño pepper Jack cheese, shredded (1 cup; avoid packaged, pre-grated versions)

skewers, as needed

1   Prepare outdoor grill for direct grilling over medium-high heat.

2   In cup, combine chili powder, 2 tablespoons oil, and ½ teaspoon salt; set chili oil aside. In bowl, combine cilantro, lime juice, and remaining ¼ teaspoon salt and 1 tablespoon oil; set aside.

3   Place poblano and corn on hot grill rack. Grill until poblano is blistered and corn is charred, 10 to 12 minutes, turning occasionally. Remove poblano; wrap in foil and set aside 15 minutes. Transfer corn to cutting board.

4   Push skewer horizontally through each onion slice. Brush both sides of onion and zucchini slices and cut sides of tomatoes with chili oil; place on hot grill rack. Grill onion and zucchini until tender, about 10 minutes, turning over once. Grill tomatoes until slightly softened, 6 to 8 minutes, turning over once. As vegetables are done, remove to platter and keep warm.

5   Unwrap poblano; cut off stem. Cut poblano lengthwise in half; peel off skin and discard seeds, then cut into ¼-inch-wide strips. Cut corn kernels from cobs; add to cilantro mixture.

6   Assemble stacks: Remove skewers from onion slices. On each of 4 dinner plates, place a tomato half, cut side up; distribute all of zucchini on top of tomatoes, then half of cheese. Arrange onion slice on top of each stack, separating onion into rings; sprinkle with remaining cheese, then with poblano strips. Top with corn mixture.

EACH SERVING: ABOUT 340 CALORIES | 13G PROTEIN | 31G CARBOHYDRATE | 21G TOTAL FAT (8G SATURATED) | 6G FIBER | 30MG CHOLESTEROL | 670MG SODIUM ☺

Ratatouille
ON THE GRILL

Traditional Provençal ratatouille is a mélange of best-of-summer vegetables slowly simmered in olive oil. Our version is quicker and packs less of a caloric punch, since the veggies are lightly brushed with a vinaigrette mixture, not braised in oil. If you have leftover ratatouille, chop it and toss it with your favorite gluten-free pasta, or layer it between two slices of Homemade Sandwich Bread (page 29), top with some fresh mozzarella, and toast in a panini press or skillet.

ACTIVE TIME: 20 MINUTES   **TOTAL TIME:** 30 MINUTES   **MAKES:** 8 MAIN-DISH SERVINGS

3   tablespoons red wine vinegar

1   garlic clove, crushed with garlic press

³/₄   teaspoon salt

¹/₄   teaspoon ground black pepper

¹/₄   cup olive oil

2   pounds plum tomatoes, cut lengthwise in half

2   red peppers, each cut lengthwise into quarters

2   medium zucchini (8 ounces each), cut crosswise into ¹/₂-inch-thick slices

1   large eggplant (1¹/₂ pounds), cut crosswise into ¹/₂-inch-thick slices

1   large onion (12 ounces), cut into ¹/₂-inch-thick slices

¹/₂   cup loosely packed fresh basil leaves, chopped

2   ounces Parmesan cheese

1   Prepare outdoor grill for covered direct grilling over medium heat.

2   Prepare vinaigrette: In small bowl, whisk together vinegar, garlic, salt, and pepper. In slow, steady stream, whisk in oil until blended.

3   On two jelly-roll pans, lightly brush tomato halves, peppers, zucchini, eggplant, and onion slices with some vinaigrette. With tongs, transfer vegetables to hot grill grate. Cover grill and cook until all vegetables are tender and lightly charred on both sides. Cook tomatoes about 6 minutes; peppers, zucchini, and eggplant about 8 minutes; and onion about 12 minutes. Return cooked vegetables to jelly-roll pans.

4   To serve, arrange grilled vegetables on platter; drizzle with remaining vinaigrette and sprinkle with basil. With vegetable peeler, shave Parmesan into large pieces over vegetables.

EACH SERVING: ABOUT 155 CALORIES | 4G PROTEIN | 16G CARBOHYDRATE | 10G TOTAL FAT (3G SATURATED) | 5G FIBER | 8MG CHOLESTEROL | 320MG SODIUM

Chicken & Apple
Meat Loaves (page 99)

6 Bakes & Casseroles

Warm your body and soul with richly flavored dinners that may take a little more time but are worth the investment for their substantive and satisfying pleasures. Whether you're cooking up a perfect dinner for two on a leisurely weekend evening, preparing a welcoming meal for treasured friends, or a fixing a homey sit-down with your family, we've got you covered with oven-baked main dishes like Mushroom-Glazed Pork Chops or Roasted Cod with Potatoes & Kale that will gratify anyone at the table.

Also included are recipes that are healthy for reasons that go beyond gluten-free. Our Stuffed Acorn Squash, brimming with a pancetta, pine nut, wild rice, and cannellini bean filling, is a hearty, low-calorie meal in a mostly-edible bowl, while Almond-Crusted Tilapia provides a flavorful dinner of lean fish packed with heart-healthy omega-3 fatty acids.

Espresso-Balsamic Roasted Chicken 96

Herbed Skillet Chicken 98

Chicken & Apple Meat Loaves 99

Mushroom-Glazed Pork Chops 100

New Orleans Pork & Charred Beans 103

Almond-Crusted Tilapia 104

Roasted Cod with Potatoes & Kale 105

Chipotle-Orange-Glazed Salmon 107

Homemade Pizza 108

Polenta & Spinach Gratin 110

Stuffed Acorn Squash 111

ESPRESSO-BALSAMIC
Roasted Chicken

Impress the table with this tangy, yet surprisingly simple glaze.
The sweet undertones of balsamic vinegar are brought out by a dash
of brown sugar. No instant espresso powder in the pantry?
Swap in a quarter-cup of brewed java.

ACTIVE TIME: 25 MINUTES   **TOTAL TIME:** 1 HOUR   **MAKES:** 6 MAIN-DISH SERVINGS

1   pound red potatoes, cut into 1-inch chunks

2   large carrots, sliced

1   medium red onion, cut into 8 wedges

1   tablespoon vegetable oil

1/2 teaspoon dried oregano

salt and ground black pepper

1   cut-up chicken (3 1/2 pounds)

1/3 cup balsamic vinegar

3   tablespoons brown sugar

2   teaspoons instant espresso powder

1/4 cup water

chopped parsley, for garnish

1 Preheat oven to 425°F.

2 In large roasting pan, toss vegetables with oil and 1/4 teaspoon oregano, salt, and pepper. Pat chicken dry with paper towel; place on top of vegetables and sprinkle with 1/2 teaspoon salt. Roast 20 minutes.

3 Meanwhile, in 2-quart saucepan, stir vinegar, sugar, espresso powder, water, remaining 1/4 teaspoon oregano, 1/8 teaspoon salt, and 1/4 teaspoon pepper. Heat to boiling on medium-high, stirring. Reduce heat; simmer 8 to 10 minutes or until thickened and slightly syrupy.

4 Brush chicken with sauce and roast 15 minutes. Brush with sauce again; roast 10 minutes or until thermometer inserted into thickest part reaches 165°F.

5 Transfer chicken and vegetables to platter. Strain pan juices into measuring cup; discard fat. Pour juices over chicken and vegetables. Garnish with parsley.

EACH SERVING: ABOUT 435 CALORIES | 35G PROTEIN | 26G CARBOHYDRATE | 21G TOTAL FAT (5G SATURATED) | 2G FIBER | 104MG CHOLESTEROL | 475MG SODIUM
☺ ♥

HERBED
Skillet Chicken

Just throw mushrooms, onions, herbs, and chicken together into a pan and let the oven do all the hard work for you.

ACTIVE TIME: 50 MINUTES   **TOTAL TIME:** 1 HOUR   **MAKES:** 4 MAIN-DISH SERVINGS

1	pound white mushrooms, halved
1	small red onion, cut into 8 wedges
2	tablespoons olive oil
1	teaspoon fresh thyme leaves
4	chicken leg quarters
1	teaspoon salt
½	teaspoon ground black pepper

1 Preheat oven to 450°F.

2 In a 12-inch cast-iron or heavy skillet, stir together mushrooms, onions, olive oil, and thyme. Top with the chicken and sprinkle salt and pepper over the entire mixture.

3 Roast in the preheated oven for 35 to 40 minutes or until cooked through (165°F).

EACH SERVING: ABOUT 625 CALORIES | 66G PROTEIN | 6G CARBOHYDRATE | 37G TOTAL FAT (9G SATURATED) | 3G FIBER | 333MG CHOLESTEROL | 841MG SODIUM

CHICKEN & APPLE
Meat Loaves

Easy-to-prepare chicken meat loaves spiced with fennel seeds, parsley, and brushed with an apple jelly and mustard sauce make for a scrumptious and calorie- and fat-saving main dish. For photo, see page 94.

ACTIVE TIME: 25 MINUTES   **TOTAL TIME:** 1 HOUR   **MAKES:** 4 MAIN-DISH SERVINGS

1   slice gluten-free whole-grain bread or Homemade Sandwich Bread (page 29)

¼   cup low-fat (1%) milk

4   medium Golden Delicious apples

1   pound ground dark-meat chicken

½   cup finely chopped onion

¼   cup packed fresh flat-leaf parsley leaves, finely chopped

1   large egg, lightly beaten

1½   teaspoons fennel seeds

½   teaspoon salt

½   teaspoon ground black pepper

1   tablespoon vegetable oil

¼   cup apple jelly

1   tablespoon Dijon mustard (Grey Poupon® brand is gluten-free)

steamed green beans, for serving (optional)

1   Preheat oven to 450°F. In food processor with knife blade attached, pulse bread into fine crumbs. Transfer to large bowl and stir in milk; let soak. Meanwhile, grate half of 1 apple on large holes of box grater. Cut remaining apple half and 3 whole apples into wedges, removing and discarding cores; set aside.

2   To bowl with crumbs, add chicken, onion, parsley, egg, grated apple, ½ teaspoon fennel seeds, salt, and pepper. With hands, mix until well combined. Divide mixture into 4 equal pieces. On 18" by 12" jelly-roll pan, form each piece into a 4½" by 2½" loaf, spacing loaves 3 inches apart.

3   In large bowl, toss apple wedges, oil, and remaining 1 teaspoon fennel seeds; scatter in even layer around meat loaves. Roast 10 minutes.

4   Meanwhile, stir together jelly and mustard until well blended. Brush or spoon thick layer of mixture onto meat loaves. Roast 10 minutes longer or until tops are browned and temperature on meat thermometer inserted into center of loaves registers 165°F. Transfer apples and meat loaves to serving plates. Serve with green beans, if desired.

EACH SERVING: ABOUT 380 CALORIES | 27G PROTEIN | 44G CARBOHYDRATE | 11G TOTAL FAT (2G SATURATED) | 6G FIBER | 145MG CHOLESTEROL | 515MG SODIUM
☺ ♥ ☻

MUSHROOM-GLAZED
Pork Chops

These golden-crusted chops are quick-seared on the stove, roasted in a roaring oven, and topped with a silky cognac-and-cream sauce.

ACTIVE TIME: 20 MINUTES   **TOTAL TIME:** 40 MINUTES   **MAKES:** 4 MAIN-DISH SERVINGS

10 ounces cremini mushrooms, trimmed and quartered

8 ounces fresh shiitake mushrooms, stems discarded, cut into 1-inch pieces if large

2 garlic cloves, very thinly sliced

1 teaspoon sugar

1 tablespoon plus 1 teaspoon sherry vinegar

½ teaspoon ground black pepper

1 tablespoon vegetable oil

4 boneless center-cut pork loin chops (6 ounces each, 1-inch thick)

1 medium onion (6 to 8 ounces), finely chopped

¼ cup cognac

¼ cup light cream

½ teaspoon salt

2 fresh sage leaves, thinly sliced

1 Arrange racks in upper and lower thirds of oven. Preheat oven to 450°F.

2 In 15½" by 10½" jelly-roll pan, spread mushrooms in even layer. Sprinkle garlic on top. Roast on upper rack 15 minutes or until mushrooms are tender, juices are released, and garlic is golden brown.

3 Meanwhile, in 9-inch pie plate or other shallow dish, mix sugar, 1 tablespoon vinegar, and ¼ teaspoon pepper. Add pork and turn to evenly coat.

4 Heat 12-inch ovenproof skillet over medium-high heat. Add oil to pan and swirl to coat bottom. When oil shimmers and is almost smoking, add pork. Cook 1 to 2 minutes or until browned; turn pork over and cook 2 minutes longer. Transfer pan to lower oven rack. Roast 7 to 10 minutes or until barely pink in center. Transfer to plate; let rest.

5 To same skillet, add onion. Cook over medium heat 5 minutes or until browned, stirring occasionally. Add cognac and remaining 1 teaspoon vinegar and cook 30 seconds. Add mushroom mixture with juices; reduce heat to low. While stirring, add cream in slow, steady stream. Stir in salt and remaining ¼ teaspoon pepper. When mixture bubbles, remove from heat.

6 Divide pork chops and their juices among serving plates. Spoon mushroom mixture over pork and garnish with sage.

EACH SERVING: ABOUT 430 CALORIES | 39G PROTEIN | 17G CARBOHYDRATE | 22G TOTAL FAT (7G SATURATED) | 2G FIBER | 127MG CHOLESTEROL | 400MG SODIUM

NEW ORLEANS
Pork & Charred Beans

This is one recipe sure to spice up your dinner routine. The pork chops are rubbed with a blend of Cajun seasonings before being broiled and served with a side of charred green beans. To shave 5 minutes off the prep time, use pre-trimmed French beans (haricots verts).

ACTIVE TIME: 15 MINUTES   **TOTAL TIME:** 30 MINUTES   **MAKES:** 4 MAIN-DISH SERVINGS

2   teaspoons hot paprika

1   teaspoon garlic powder

1   teaspoon dried oregano

3/4 teaspoon salt

1/4 teaspoon cayenne (ground red) pepper

4   thin-cut, bone-in pork chops

4   teaspoons olive oil

1   pound green beans

2   tablespoons water

1 Preheat broiler. In a small bowl, mix paprika, garlic powder, oregano, ½ tsp salt, and cayenne pepper.

2 Brush pork chops with 2 teaspoons oil and then rub them with the spice mixture. Transfer the pork chops to a foil-lined jelly-roll pan. Broil the pork chops, 6 inches from the heat source, on high for 5 minutes.

3 Meanwhile, microwave green beans and water in a covered baking dish on high for 2 minutes, or until the beans are bright green. Drain the green beans and toss them with 2 teaspoons of olive oil and ¼ teaspoon salt.

4 Remove the pork chops from the oven, flip them, and push them to one side of the pan. Spread the green beans on the other side of pan and broil for 3 minutes, or until the beans blister and the pork is cooked to 145°F. Serve with the pan juices.

EACH SERVING: ABOUT 295 CALORIES | 23G PROTEIN | 9G CARBOHYDRATE | 19G TOTAL FAT (6G SATURATED) | 4G FIBER | 61MG CHOLESTEROL | 485MG SODIUM

ALMOND-CRUSTED
Tilapia

Skip the breadcrumbs: Here, mild-mannered tilapia is topped with a crunchy coating of almond slices instead. A medley of green beans and mushrooms completes the meal.

ACTIVE TIME: 15 MINUTES   **TOTAL TIME:** 30 MINUTES   **MAKES:** 4 MAIN-DISH SERVINGS

2 to 3 lemons

2   tablespoons olive oil

½   teaspoon salt

¼   teaspoon ground black pepper

4   tilapia fillets (6 ounces each)

¼   cup sliced natural almonds

1   small onion (4 to 6 ounces), chopped

1   bag (12 ounces) trimmed fresh green beans

1   package (10 ounces) sliced white mushrooms

2   tablespoons water

1 Preheat oven to 425°F. From 1 or 2 lemons, grate 1 teaspoon peel and squeeze 3 tablespoons juice; cut remaining lemon into wedges. In cup, mix lemon peel and 1 tablespoon juice, 1 tablespoon oil, ¼ teaspoon salt, and ⅛ teaspoon pepper.

2 Spray 13" by 9" baking dish with nonstick cooking spray; place tilapia, dark side down, in dish. Drizzle tilapia with lemon mixture; press almonds on top. Bake 15 minutes or until just opaque throughout.

3 Meanwhile, in 12-inch skillet, heat remaining 1 tablespoon oil over medium-high heat, 1 minute. Add onion and cook 5 to 6 minutes or until golden, stirring occasionally. Stir in green beans, mushrooms, water, and remaining ¼ teaspoon salt and ⅛ teaspoon pepper. Cook about 6 minutes or until most of liquid evaporates and green beans are tender-crisp. Toss with remaining 2 tablespoons lemon juice. Serve bean mixture and lemon wedges alongside tilapia.

EACH SERVING: ABOUT 315 CALORIES | 33G PROTEIN | 15G CARBOHYDRATE | 15G TOTAL FAT (1G SATURATED) | 5G FIBER | 0MG CHOLESTEROL | 380MG SODIUM

Roasted Cod
WITH POTATOES & KALE

This good-for-you recipe features lean cod atop a mixture of
dark green kale and mashed potatoes.

ACTIVE TIME: 15 MINUTES   **TOTAL TIME:** 35 MINUTES   **MAKES:** 4 MAIN-DISH SERVINGS

1   package (10 ounces) frozen chopped kale

1   package (16 ounces) frozen mashed potatoes

2   slices bacon (Smith's®, Hormel™, and Oscar Meyer® offer gluten-free options; see Tip, page 44), cut crosswise into ½-inch-wide pieces

1   pound cod or scrod fillet, 1-inch thick, cut into 4 pieces

¼   teaspoon salt

2   tablespoons cornmeal (Certified Gluten-Free Bob's Red Mill® and Arrowhead Mills® brands are guaranteed gluten-free)

1   large onion (12 ounces), thinly sliced

½   cup gluten-free chicken broth, such as Swanson®

2   teaspoons cider vinegar

1   In microwave oven, cook kale, then heat potatoes as package labels direct. Drain kale. In medium bowl, stir kale and potatoes together until blended. Cover and keep warm.

2   Preheat oven to 450°F. Meanwhile, in nonstick 12-inch skillet, cook bacon over medium heat until browned. With slotted spoon, remove bacon to paper towels to drain. Discard bacon fat.

3   On waxed paper, sprinkle cod with salt, then cornmeal, turning to coat. In same skillet, over medium-high heat, cook cod about 2 minutes per side or until lightly browned. Transfer cod to pie plate; place in oven and roast cod 8 to 10 minutes or until opaque throughout. Leave skillet on stove and reduce heat to medium.

4   Add onion to skillet. Cook, covered, 5 minutes or until onion is browned, stirring once. Add broth; cover and cook 4 minutes to wilt onion. Remove from heat; stir in vinegar and bacon.

5   To serve, reheat potato mixture in microwave oven if necessary. Spoon potato mixture onto four dinner plates; top with cod, then onion mixture.

EACH SERVING: ABOUT 315 CALORIES | 28G PROTEIN | 31G CARBOHYDRATE | 9G TOTAL FAT (4G SATURATED) | 5G FIBER | 67MG CHOLESTEROL | 845MG SODIUM
☺ ♥ ❀

CHIPOTLE-ORANGE-GLAZED
Salmon

Canned chipotle chiles come packed in their own flavorful adobo sauce, which adds a smoky kick to the orange-glazed salmon.

ACTIVE TIME: 25 MINUTES   **TOTAL TIME:** 40 MINUTES   **MAKES:** 4 MAIN-DISH SERVINGS

1   orange

1   chipotle chile in adobo sauce, plus 2 teaspoons adobo sauce

1   clove garlic, peeled

1/2   teaspoon ground cumin

1   cup quinoa, cooked according to package directions

1   bunch radishes, trimmed, halved, and thinly sliced

1/2   cup fresh corn kernels (from 1 ear)

1/2   cup fresh cilantro leaves, chopped

2   green onions, sliced

salt

4   skinless salmon fillets (5 ounces each)

1   Arrange oven rack 4 to 6 inches from broiler heat source. Preheat broiler on high. Line jelly-roll pan with foil.

2   Meanwhile, from orange, grate 1 teaspoon peel and squeeze 1/2 cup juice. In blender, puree chipotle chile, adobo sauce, garlic, cumin, and orange juice.

3   Add quinoa into a medium bowl, stirring in radishes, corn, cilantro, green onions, orange peel, and 1/8 teaspoon salt.

4   Arrange salmon on prepared pan. Sprinkle with 1/8 teaspoon salt, then brush generously on all sides with chile mixture. Broil 5 to 7 minutes or until just opaque throughout. Serve salmon on quinoa pilaf.

EACH SERVING: ABOUT 365 CALORIES | 36G PROTEIN | 35G CARBOHYDRATE | 8G TOTAL FAT (2G SATURATED) | 4G FIBER | 66MG CHOLESTEROL | 240 MG SODIUM
☺ ♥

HOMEMADE **Pizza**

This gluten-free pizza crust is crisp and satisfying. Enjoy it with our simple tomato sauce, mozzarella, and basil topping, or load it up with broccoli, roasted red peppers, and Kalamata olives, as shown here.

ACTIVE TIME: 35 MINUTES   **TOTAL TIME:** 1 HOUR PLUS RISING   **MAKES:** 2 PIZZAS OR 8 MAIN-DISH SERVINGS

2½ cups All-Purpose Flour Blend (page 114) or gluten-free all-purpose flour

½ cup brown rice flour

½ cup millet flour

1 tablespoon packed brown sugar

1 tablespoon xanthan gum (see Tip, page 23)

1 package quick-rise yeast

1 teaspoon salt

1 cup very warm water (120° to 130°F)

1 large egg, at room temperature

2 tablespoons olive oil

gluten-free cornmeal, for sprinkling in pan

1 cup marinara sauce

8 ounces fresh mozzarella cheese, thinly sliced

¼ cup fresh basil leaves, torn

1 In food processor, combine flour blend, brown rice flour, millet flour, brown sugar, xanthan gum, yeast, and salt. Process to blend.

2 In 2-cup glass measuring cup, combine warm water, egg, and oil. With motor running, pour into food processor. Process 1 minute. Mixture will be soft and sticky, a batter rather than a dough. Scrape into medium bowl. Cover with plastic wrap and let stand 15 minutes.

3 Preheat oven to 450°F. Grease two 12-inch cast-iron pans or heavy baking sheets; sprinkle with cornmeal. Turn dough out onto floured surface and divide in half. Place 1 piece dough in each prepared pan. Using wet hands, press to flatten and spread each into 11-inch circles. Because dough is soft and sticky, rinse hands often. Bake 12 to 14 minutes or until golden brown around edges, rotating pans on oven racks halfway through.

4 Remove crusts from oven and spread with marinara sauce up to ½-inch from edges. Top with mozzarella and other desired toppings. Bake 10 minutes or until crusts brown and cheese melts, rotating pans on oven racks halfway through. Sprinkle with basil.

EACH SERVING: ABOUT 350 CALORIES | 10G PROTEIN | 51G CARBOHYDRATE | 12G TOTAL FAT (5G SATURATED) | 5G FIBER | 46MG CHOLESTEROL | 454MG SODIUM

☺ ♥ ☘

POLENTA & SPINACH
Gratin

A creamy spinach topping is layered over slices of ready-made polenta for a comforting side dish or vegetarian entrée. You can assemble this casserole completely up to one day ahead, but do not bake it. Cover and refrigerate overnight, then bake in a reheated 425°F oven until hot and bubbly, about 40 minutes.

ACTIVE TIME: 20 MINUTES   **TOTAL TIME:** 55 MINUTES   **MAKES:** 16 SIDE-DISH OR 10 MAIN-DISH SERVINGS

- 2   logs (24 ounces each) precooked plain polenta
- 2   tablespoons olive oil
- 1   large onion, chopped
- 2   garlic cloves, minced
- ¼   teaspoon crushed red pepper
- 3   packages (10 ounces each) frozen chopped spinach, thawed and squeezed dry
- 3½ cups whole milk
- 2   tablespoons gluten-free cornstarch (see Tip, page 17)
- 1   teaspoon salt
- 1   cup freshly grated Parmesan cheese

1 Preheat oven to 425°F. Cut each polenta log crosswise in half, then cut each half lengthwise into 6 slices. In 13" by 9" ceramic or glass baking dish, place half of polenta slices, overlapping slightly.

2 In 4-quart saucepan, heat oil over medium heat until hot. Add onion and cook until tender and golden, 10 to 12 minutes, stirring occasionally. Add garlic and crushed red pepper and cook 1 minute, stirring. Add spinach and cook 3 minutes to heat through, stirring frequently and separating spinach with fork.

3 In medium bowl, with wire whisk, mix milk and cornstarch. Stir in salt and all but 2 tablespoons Parmesan. Add milk mixture to spinach mixture in saucepan; heat to boiling over medium-high heat. Reduce heat to low; cook 2 minutes, stirring occasionally. Remove saucepan from heat.

4 Spoon half of spinach mixture over polenta slices in baking dish. Repeat layering with remaining polenta slices and spinach mixture. Sprinkle with reserved Parmesan. Bake until hot and bubbly, about 20 minutes.

EACH SIDE-DISH SERVING: ABOUT 155 CALORIES | 8G PROTEIN | 19G CARBOHYDRATE | 5G TOTAL FAT (3G SATURATED) | 2G FIBER | 12MG CHOLESTEROL | 625MG SODIUM 🍲

STUFFED
Acorn Squash

To make this a hearty vegetarian main dish, omit the pancetta. Or serve it as a side with roast turkey or chicken. If you have trouble locating gluten-free pancetta, swap in four slices of cooked bacon, crumbled.

ACTIVE TIME: 35 MINUTES   **TOTAL TIME:** 55 MINUTES   **MAKES:** 4 MAIN-DISH SERVINGS

- 2 acorn squash (1½ pounds each), cut in half and seeded
- 1 teaspoon olive oil
- 2 ounces pancetta (Boar's Head® Old World Delicacies Diced Pancetta is gluten-free), finely chopped
- 1 small onion (4 to 6 ounces), finely chopped
- 2 large stalks celery, finely chopped
- ⅛ teaspoon crushed red pepper
- ¼ teaspoon salt
- ¼ teaspoon ground black pepper
- 1 can (15 ounces) low-sodium white kidney (cannellini) beans
- ¼ cup water
- 1 package (7 to 8 ounces) heat-and-serve precooked wild rice; do not heat
- 4 teaspoons pine nuts (pignoli)
- ½ cup packed fresh basil leaves, thinly sliced

1 Preheat oven to 375°F. Line 15½" by 10½" jelly-roll pan with foil. On large microwave-safe plate, arrange squash halves in single layer, cut sides down. Microwave on high 9 to 11 minutes or until knife pierces flesh easily.

2 Meanwhile, in 12-inch skillet, heat oil over medium-high heat until hot. Add pancetta and cook 3 to 4 minutes or until browned and crisp, stirring frequently. With slotted spoon, transfer to paper towels to drain. To drippings in skillet, add onion, celery, crushed red pepper, salt, and black pepper. Cook, stirring frequently, 4 to 5 minutes or until vegetables are tender and golden brown. Remove from heat. In small bowl, mash ¼ cup beans with water. Into vegetables in skillet, stir rice, mashed beans, whole beans, pancetta, 2 teaspoons pine nuts, and half of basil.

3 On prepared jelly-roll pan, arrange squash halves in single layer, cut side up. Divide bean mixture among squash cavities, pressing firmly into cavities and mounding on top. Cover pan with foil. Bake 15 minutes. Uncover and bake 5 to 7 minutes longer or until squash and vegetables are golden on top. Garnish with remaining pine nuts and basil.

EACH SERVING: ABOUT 350 CALORIES | 13G PROTEIN | 59G CARBOHYDRATE | 9G TOTAL FAT (3G SATURATED) | 12G FIBER | 7MG CHOLESTEROL | 330MG SODIUM
☺ ♥ ⊛

Flourless Chocolate-Hazelnut Cake (page 120)

7 Sweet & Fruity Finales

No need to deprive yourself of dessert! There are plenty of gluten-free options when it comes to delectable treats—including yummy gluten-free baked goods—and this chapter provides an enticing variety to choose from.

Chocolate, for starters, is naturally gluten-free, although that doesn't make all chocolate products problem-free, and it's wise to exercise caution. (When buying chocolate, it's best to give preference to products that are labeled gluten-free.) Indulge your sweet tooth with luscious treats like our Drunken Chocolate Figs and Flourless Chocolate-Hazelnut Cake, a gooey gateau that combines melted chocolate and butter with eggs beaten until they triple in volume with a pretty praline candy shard topping. For a fruity turn, satisfy your sweet yearnings with delectable treats like Lemon Meringue Drops that will melt in your mouth, and Banana-Berry Parfaits that you can whip up in the time it takes to throw fruit and yogurt into a blender.

All-Purpose Flour Blend 114

Oatmeal-Chocolate Chip Cookies 115

Peanut Butter Cookies 116

Lemon Meringue Drops 117

Pumpkin Crème Caramel 119

Flourless Chocolate-Hazelnut Cake 120

Drunken Chocolate Figs 121

Banana-Berry Parfaits 122

ALL-PURPOSE
Flour Blend

This gluten-free flour blend is used in multiple baked goods in this book—from pizza crust to cookies—so it's well worth the effort to mix up a batch and keep it on hand. For a shortcut, you can swap in a commercial all-purpose flour blend: King Arthur®, Arrowhead Mills®, Bob's Red Mill®, and Gluten Free Pantry® brands all offer gluten-free options. The ingredients vary, so they'll yield different results. Experiment until you find a brand you like.

TOTAL TIME: 5 MINUTES   **MAKES:** 6 CUPS

2   cups sorghum flour (see Tip)

1½ cups potato starch

1   cup tapioca flour

1   cup corn flour

In large bowl, whisk sorghum flour, potato starch, tapioca flour, and corn flour until thoroughly blended. Store in an airtight container up to 1 week.

TIP

Sorghum flour, potato starch, and tapioca flour are available at health-food stores or health-oriented supermarkets such as Whole Foods®. If you have trouble locating them, ask your local health-food store to order them, or purchase them online.

EACH ½ CUP: ABOUT 230 CALORIES | 4G PROTEIN | 53G CARBOHYDRATE | 1G TOTAL FAT (0G SATURATED) | 4G FIBER | 0MG CHOLESTEROL | 0MG SODIUM

OATMEAL–CHOCOLATE CHIP
Cookies

If oatmeal cookies are your favorite cookie jar-filler, don't despair:
We've created a gluten-free version—studded with chocolate chips—
that's as moist and chewy as the classic. However, a small
portion of people with celiac disease cannot tolerate oats,
even those labeled gluten-free.

ACTIVE TIME: 30 MINUTES   **BAKE TIME:** 12 MINUTES PER BATCH PLUS COOLING
MAKES: 36 COOKIES

2   cups All-Purpose Flour Blend (page 114),
    or gluten-free all-purpose flour

1   teaspoon baking soda

1/2 teaspoon salt

1/2 teaspoon xanthan gum, optional
    (see Tip, page 23)

3/4 cup butter (1 1/2 sticks), softened

3/4 cup packed brown sugar

1/2 cup granulated sugar

2   large eggs

1   teaspoon vanilla extract (McCormick®,
    Spice Islands®, and Durkee® are gluten-free)

2   cups quick-cooking gluten-free oats, such as
    Bob's Red Mill®

1   cup chocolate chips (Nestlé Toll House®
    brand is gluten-free)

1   cup walnuts, chopped

1 Preheat oven to 375°F. Grease three large
baking sheets with nonstick cooking spray (avoid
baking spray, which typically contains flour).

2 In medium bowl, whisk together flour blend,
baking soda, salt, and xanthan gum, if using.

3 In large bowl, with mixer on low speed, beat
butter, brown sugar, and granulated sugar
until smooth and fluffy. Beat in eggs one at
a time. Beat in vanilla. Beat in flour mixture
until blended. Stir in oats, chocolate chips, and
walnuts.

4 Drop dough by heaping measuring tablespoons
onto prepared baking sheets, spacing cookies
2 inches apart. Bake one sheet at a time for 12
minutes or until cookies are firm and golden
brown. Let stand on baking sheet 1 minute
before removing with spatula to wire rack to cool
completely.

EACH COOKIE: ABOUT 155 CALORIES | 2G PROTEIN |
20G CARBOHYDRATE | 8G TOTAL FAT (4G SATURATED) |
1G FIBER | 21MG CHOLESTEROL | 107MG SODIUM

PEANUT BUTTER
Cookies

Nothing beats a plate of warm peanut butter cookies with a glass of cold milk. We invite you to sink your teeth into our take on these old-fashioned favorites, made with natural peanut butter and our easy gluten-free flour blend.

ACTIVE TIME: 35 MINUTES **BAKE TIME:** 12 MINUTES PER BATCH PLUS COOLING
MAKES: 24 COOKIES

1   cup All-Purpose Flour Blend (page 114), or gluten-free all-purpose flour

¼   cup gluten-free cornstarch (see Tip, page 17)

1   teaspoon baking powder

1   teaspoon baking soda

½   teaspoon salt

1   cup natural creamy peanut butter (see Tip)

4   tablespoons butter, softened

½   cup packed brown sugar

½   cup granulated sugar

2   large eggs

1   teaspoon vanilla extract (McCormick®, Spice Islands®, and Durkee® are gluten-free)

1 Preheat oven to 350°F. Grease two large baking sheets with cooking spray (avoid baking spray, which typically contains flour). In small bowl, whisk together flour blend, cornstarch, baking powder, baking soda, and salt.

2 In large bowl, with electric mixer on low speed, beat peanut butter, butter, brown sugar, and granulated sugar until smooth and creamy. Beat in eggs one at a time until well blended. Beat in vanilla. Beat in flour mixture.

3 Using heaping measuring tablespoons, shape dough into balls and place 2 inches apart on prepared baking sheets. Press with fork. Bake one sheet at a time for 12 to 15 minutes or until cookies are golden brown at edges. Let stand on baking sheet 1 minute before removing with spatula to wire rack to cool completely.

TIP

Choosing natural peanut butter, which is made exclusively from nuts and oil, ensures that the product is gluten-free and avoids added sugar, too. One nationally available brand is Arrowhead Mills®. It produces a range of nut butters, from peanut butter to almond and cashew butters, and natural tahini (sesame seed paste).

EACH COOKIE: ABOUT 150 CALORIES | 3G PROTEIN | 17G CARBOHYDRATE | 8G TOTAL FAT (2G SATURATED) | 1G FIBER | 21MG CHOLESTEROL | 188MG SODIUM
♥ ☺ 🍴

LEMON
Meringue Drops

These melt-in-your-mouth meringues are both crunchy and cloud-light—
and require only five ingredients.

ACTIVE TIME: 45 MINUTES   **BAKE TIME:** 1 HOUR 30 MINUTES PLUS 1 HOUR STANDING
MAKES: 60 COOKIES

3   large egg whites

¼   teaspoon cream of tartar

⅛   teaspoon salt

½   cup sugar

2   teaspoons freshly grated lemon peel

1 Preheat oven to 200°F. Line two baking sheets with parchment paper.

2 In medium bowl, with mixer at high speed, beat egg whites, cream of tartar, and salt until soft peaks form. With mixer running, sprinkle in sugar, 2 tablespoons at a time, beating until sugar dissolves and meringue stands in stiff, glossy peaks when beaters are lifted. Gently fold in lemon peel.

3 Spoon meringue into decorating bag fitted with ½-inch star tip. Pipe meringue into 1½-inch stars, about 1 inch apart, on prepared cookie sheets.

4 Bake meringues until crisp but not brown, 1 hour 30 minutes, rotating cookie sheets between upper and lower racks halfway through baking. Turn oven off; leave meringues in oven until dry, 1 hour.

5 Remove meringues from oven and cool completely. Remove from parchment with wide metal spatula. Store in tightly sealed container at room temperature up to 1 month.

....

EACH COOKIE: ABOUT 5 CALORIES | 0G PROTEIN | 2G CARBOHYDRATE | 0G TOTAL FAT (0G SATURATED) | 0G FIBER | 0MG CHOLESTEROL | 10MG SODIUM ☺ ♥ 📷

PUMPKIN
Crème Caramel

This showstopping crème caramel is perfect for the holiday table. Since there's no crust, it's 100-percent gluten-free.

ACTIVE TIME: 15 MINUTES   **TOTAL TIME:** 1 HOUR 5 MINUTES PLUS CHILLING   **MAKES:** 12 SERVINGS

¼ cup water

1¼ cups sugar

1 can (14 ounces) coconut milk (not cream of coconut), well-shaken

¾ cup heavy or whipping cream

1 cup solid pack pumpkin (not pumpkin pie mix)

6 large eggs

2 teaspoons vanilla extract (McCormick®, Spice Islands®, and Durkee® are gluten-free)

⅛ teaspoon salt

freshly whipped cream, toasted coarsely shredded coconut, and grated nutmeg, for garnish

1 Preheat oven to 350°F. In 1-quart saucepan, heat water and ¾ cup sugar to boiling over medium-high heat, stirring to dissolve sugar. Continue to cook, without stirring, 5 to 9 minutes or until caramel is just amber in color. Pour caramel into 9-inch-round, 2-inch-deep ceramic or metal pan, swirling to evenly coat bottom of pan.

2 In 2-quart saucepan, heat coconut milk, heavy cream, and remaining ½ cup sugar just to boiling over medium-high heat, stirring to dissolve sugar.

3 Meanwhile, in large bowl, with wire whisk, mix pumpkin, eggs, vanilla, and salt until blended.

4 Whisk hot coconut milk mixture into pumpkin mixture until blended. Pour pumpkin mixture through sieve into 8-cup glass measuring cup, then into caramel-coated pan. Place pan in roasting pan; place on oven rack. Pour *boiling water* into roasting pan to come three-quarters of the way up the side of 9-inch pan. Bake 45 to 55 minutes (if using metal pan, start checking for doneness at 35 minutes) or until knife comes out clean when inserted 1 inch from edge of custard (center will still jiggle slightly).

5 Carefully remove pan from water. Allow crème caramel to cool 1 hour in pan on wire rack. Cover and refrigerate overnight or up to 2 days. To unmold, run a small spatula around side of pan; invert crème caramel onto serving plate, allowing caramel syrup to drip down from pan. Garnish with a dollop of whipped cream, coconut, and nutmeg.

....

EACH SERVING: ABOUT 240 CALORIES | 5G PROTEIN | 24G CARBOHYDRATE | 15G TOTAL FAT (11G SATURATED) | 1G FIBER | 125MG CHOLESTEROL | 70MG SODIUM 🍲

FLOURLESS
Chocolate-Hazelnut Cake

You'll love the truffle-like creaminess of this cake, and the hazelnut-praline topping is sure to elicit oohs and ahs.
For photo, see page 112.

ACTIVE TIME: 30 MINUTES **TOTAL TIME:** 1 HOUR 10 MINUTES **MAKES:** 12 SERVINGS

1   cup hazelnuts (filberts), toasted, peeled, and cooled

1¼   cups sugar

8   squares (8 ounces) semisweet chocolate, chopped

4   tablespoons butter

5   large eggs

¾   cup heavy or whipping cream

1   Preheat oven to 350°F. Lightly grease 9-inch springform pan. Line bottom with waxed or parchment paper; grease paper.

2   In food processor with knife blade attached, place ¾ cup nuts and ¼ cup sugar; pulse until finely ground. Set aside. With chef's knife, roughly chop remaining nuts; set aside.

3   In 3-quart saucepan, melt chocolate and butter over medium-low heat, stirring often. Meanwhile, in large bowl, with mixer on medium-high speed, beat eggs and ½ cup sugar 7 minutes or until tripled in volume. With rubber spatula, fold in chocolate mixture then ground-nut mixture. Pour batter into prepared pan and bake 35 minutes or until top is dry and cracked and toothpick inserted in center comes out slightly wet. Cool in pan on wire rack 10 minutes. Remove side of pan; cool 30 minutes longer.

4   Meanwhile, prepare praline garnish: Line 9-inch cake pan with foil. In pan, spread reserved chopped hazelnuts in single layer. In 12-inch skillet, spread remaining ½ cup sugar in even layer. Cook over medium-high heat 3 to 5 minutes or until sugar is melted and golden amber. Do not stir; swirl sugar in pan to cook evenly. Immediately drizzle melted sugar over nuts to coat evenly. Cool praline completely in pan.

5   While praline cools, in large bowl, with mixer on medium speed, beat cream until soft peaks form, 3 to 5 minutes. To serve, break praline into 12 large pieces. Cut cake and divide slices among serving plates. Top each slice with dollop of whipped cream and shard of hazelnut praline.

EACH SERVING: ABOUT 360 CALORIES | 6G PROTEIN | 33G CARBOHYDRATE | 25G TOTAL FAT (11G SATURATED) | 2G FIBER | 120MG CHOLESTEROL | 75MG SODIUM

DRUNKEN
Chocolate Figs

Dipped in dark chocolate and drizzled with a made-in-minutes port syrup, fiber-rich fresh figs are swiftly transformed into a simple-meets-sophisticated finale to summer supper.

ACTIVE TIME: 20 MINUTES **TOTAL TIME:** 25 MINUTES PLUS CHILLING AND STANDING
MAKES: 4 SERVINGS

1   cup ruby port wine

½ cup sugar

1   cinnamon stick

3   squares (3 ounces) bittersweet chocolate

12 fresh ripe green or black figs

1 In heavy-bottomed 2-quart saucepan, heat port, sugar, and cinnamon stick to boiling over high heat. Reduce heat to medium and cook 13 minutes, stirring frequently to prevent liquid from boiling over, until syrup is reduced by half. Remove from heat and cool to room temperature (syrup will thicken as it cools).

2 Meanwhile, line cookie sheet with waxed paper. Place chocolate in microwave-safe small bowl or cup and cover with waxed paper. Heat in microwave on high 1 minute or until chocolate is almost melted. Stir until smooth.

3 Holding 1 fig by stem end, dip into melted chocolate, leaving top half uncoated. Shake off excess chocolate. Place chocolate-covered fig on prepared cookie sheet. Repeat with remaining figs and chocolate.

4 Place chocolate-covered figs in refrigerator 15 minutes or until chocolate is set. If not serving right away, refrigerate figs up to 12 hours.

5 To serve, arrange figs on four dessert plates and drizzle with port syrup.

EACH SERVING: ABOUT 350 CALORIES | 3G PROTEIN | 73G CARBOHYDRATE | 8G TOTAL FAT (5G SATURATED) | 7G FIBER | 0MG CHOLESTEROL | 5MG SODIUM

BANANA-BERRY
Parfaits

This quick dessert looks sensational served in an old-fashioned sundae glass. Because flavored yogurt is sometimes made with gluten-containing additives, we offer simple instructions for flavoring plain yogurt with vanilla.

TOTAL TIME: 10 MINUTES **MAKES:** 4 SERVINGS

1¼ cups unsweetened frozen raspberries, partially thawed

1 tablespoon sugar

2⅔ cups plain nonfat yogurt

1½ teaspoons vanilla extract (McCormick®, Spice Islands®, and Durkee® are gluten-free)

2 ripe bananas, peeled and thinly sliced

fresh raspberries (optional)

1 In food processor with knife blade attached, pulse thawed raspberries and sugar until almost smooth. In a medium bowl, combine yogurt and vanilla to create homemade vanilla yogurt.

2 Into four 10-ounce glasses or goblets, layer about half of raspberry puree, half of yogurt, and half of banana slices; repeat layering. Top with fresh raspberries, if you like.

···

EACH SERVING: ABOUT 140 CALORIES | 6G PROTEIN | 30G CARBOHYDRATE | 0G TOTAL FAT (0G SATURATED) | 2G FIBER | 3MG CHOLESTEROL | 95MG SODIUM

Index

Note: Page numbers in *italics* indicate photos on pages separate from recipes.

Amaranth, about, 10
Apples
    Chicken & Apple Meat Loaves, *94*, 99
    Lentil Salad with Shrimp, Apples & Mint,
        38–39
    Morning Glory Muffins, *24–25*

Bakes & casseroles, 95–111
    about: overview of recipes, 95
    Almond-Crusted Tilapia, 104
    Chicken & Apple Meat Loaves, *94*, 99
    Chipotle-Orange-Glazed Salmon, *106–107*
    Espresso-Balsamic Roasted Chicken,
        96–97
    Herbed Skillet Chicken, 98
    Homemade Pizza, 108–*109*
    Mushroom-Glazed Pork Chops, 100–*101*
    New Orleans Pork & Charred Beans,
        102–103
    Polenta & Spinach Gratin, 110
    Roasted Cod with Potatoes & Kale, 105
    Stuffed Acorn Squash, 111
Bananas
    Banana-Berry Parfaits, *122–123*
    Banana Bread, 23
    Banana-Peanut Butter Smoothie, 14
Basil, in Fruit-Basil Salsa, *80–81*
Beans and other legumes. *See also* Green
        beans
    Edamame Salad, *90–91*
    Huevos Rancheros, *18–19*
    Lentil Salad with Shrimp, Apples & Mint,
        38–39
    Mixed Vegetable Minestrone, 47
    Rice & Bean Burgers, 28
    Six-Bean Salad with Tomato Vinaigrette,
        37
    Stuffed Acorn Squash, 111
    Valentine's Day Red Chili, 53
Beef
    Fire-Grilled Steak, *88–89*
    Healthy Makeover Beef Burgundy, *50–51*
    Korean Steak in Lettuce Cups, *86–87*
    Steak & Tomato Sauté, *68–69*
    Steaks with Green Sauce, *66–67*
    Tangerine Beef Stir-Fry, 65
Beets, in Valentine's Day Red Chili, 53
Berries
    Banana-Berry Parfaits, *122–123*
    Pomegranate-Berry Smoothie, *14–15*
Blinis, buckwheat, 22
Brazilian-Style Pork Chops, 62
Breads. *See also* Sandwiches
    about: commercially-available gluten-free,
        10
    Banana Bread, 23
    Homemade Sandwich Bread, 29
    Morning Glory Muffins, *24–25*
Breakfasts & brunches, 13–25
    about: overview of recipes, 13
    Banana Bread, 23
    Banana-Peanut Butter Smoothie, 14

Buckwheat Blinis, 22
Buckwheat Pancakes, 22
Crustless Tomato-Ricotta Pie, *12*, 17
Hazelnut & Fruit Granola, 16
Huevos Rancheros, *18–19*
Morning Glory Muffins, *24–25*
Pomegranate-Berry Smoothie, *14–15*
Potato-Crusted Quiche, *20–21*
Buckwheat, about, 10
Buckwheat Pancakes/Blinis, 22
Burgers. *See* Sandwiches

Casseroles. *See* Bakes & casseroles
Cheese
    eggs with. *See* Eggs
    Homemade Pizza, 108–*109*
    Tofu-Parmesan Croutons, 46
Cherries, in Hazelnut & Fruit Granola, 16
Chicken. *See* Poultry
Chilled Corn & Bacon Soup, *44–45*
Chipotle-Orange-Glazed Salmon, *106–107*
Chocolate
    Drunken Chocolate Figs, 121
    Flourless Chocolate Hazelnut Cake, *112*,
        120
    Oatmeal-Chocolate Chip Cookies, 115
Coconut, in Hazelnut & Fruit Granola, 16
Coffee-Spiced Chicken with Fruit-Basil Salsa,
        80–81
Coq au Riesling, *42*, 52
Corn
    about, 10–11
    Chilled Corn & Bacon Soup, *44–45*
    Mexican Veggie Stacks, 92
    Polenta & Spinach Gratin, 110
Cornstarch, gluten-free, 17
Crème caramel, pumpkin, *118–119*
Croutons, tofu-Parmesan, 46
Curried Chicken Pitas, *30–31*

Edamame, 37, 47, *90–91*
Eggplant, in Ratatouille on the Grill, 93
Eggs
    Crustless Tomato-Ricotta Pie, *12*, 17
    Huevos Rancheros, *18–19*
    Potato-Crusted Quiche, *20–21*
Espresso-Balsamic Roasted Chicken, *96–97*

Figs, drunken chocolate, 121
Figs, in Hazelnut & Fruit Granola, 16
Fire-Grilled Steak, *88–89*
Fish and seafood
    about: blue mussels/preparing mussels, 49
    Almond-Crusted Tilapia, 104
    Caramelized Chili Shrimp Stir-Fry, 71
    Chipotle-Orange-Glazed Salmon, *106–107*
    Fish Stew, *48–49*
    Home-Style Pad Thai, 64
    Lentil Salad with Shrimp, Apples & Mint,
        38–39
    Miso-Glazed Salmon with Edamame
        Salad, *90–91*
    Open-Faced Smoked Salmon Sandwiches,
        32–33
    Roasted Cod with Potatoes & Kale, 105
    Salad Niçoise, *26*, 36
    Spring Vegetable Risotto with Shrimp,
        56, 70
Flour blend, all-purpose, 114
Flourless Chocolate Hazelnut Cake, *112*, 120

Fruit. *See also specific fruit*
    Fruit-Basil Salsa, *80–81*
    Hazelnut & Fruit Granola, 16

Gluten-free diet
    buying foods for, 8–10
    commercial breads for, 10
    grains for, 10–11
    nutrition and, 8
    this book and, 7
    who benefits from, 8
Gluten, what it is, 8
Grains. *See also* Breads; Quinoa; Rice and
        wild rice; Sandwiches
    about: gluten-free types, 10–11
    All-Purpose Flour Blend, 114
Granola, hazelnut & fruit, 16
Green beans, *26*, 36, *102–103*
Greens. *See also* Salads
    Mango Chicken Lettuce Cups, *34–35*
    Polenta & Spinach Gratin, 110
    Roasted Cod with Potatoes & Kale,
        105
Green Sauce, 66
Grilled favorites, 77–93
    about: overview of recipes, 77
    Coffee-Spiced Chicken with Fruit-Basil
        Salsa, *80–81*
    Fire-Grilled Steak, *88–89*
    Jerk Pork Chops with Grilled Pineapple,
        76, 83
    Jerk Turkey Burgers, 82
    Korean Steak in Lettuce Cups, *86–87*
    Mexican Veggie Stacks, 92
    Miso-Glazed Salmon with Edamame
        Salad, *90–91*
    Ratatouille on the Grill, 93
    Sausage-Pepper Kabobs, *84–85*
    Sweet & Tangy Barbecued Chicken, *78–79*

Hazelnuts. *See* Nuts and seeds
Healthy Makeover Beef Burgundy, *50–51*
Heart-healthy recipes icon, 7
Herbed Skillet Chicken, 98
High-fiber recipes icon, 7
Huevos Rancheros, *18–19*

Icons, key to, 7

Jerk Pork Chops with Grilled Pineapple,
        76, 83
Jerk Turkey Burgers, 82

Kabobs, sausage-pepper, *84–85*
Kale, roasted cod with potatoes &, 105
Key, to icons, 7
Korean Steak in Lettuce Cups, *86–87*

Lemon Meringue Drops, 117
Lentil Salad with Shrimp, Apples, & Mint,
        38–39
Lettuce cups, *34–35*, *86–87*
Low-cal recipes icon, 7

Make-ahead recipes icon, 7
Mango Chicken Lettuce Cups, *34–35*
Meat loaves, chicken & apple, *94*, 99
Metric conversion charts, 127
Mexican Veggie Stacks, 92
Millet, about, 11

Miso-Glazed Salmon with Edamame Salad, 90–*91*
Mushrooms
    Chicken and Mushrooms with Brown Rice, *60*–61
    Mushroom-Glazed Pork Chops, 100–*101*
    Steak & Tomato Sauté, *68*–69

New Orleans Pork & Charred Beans, *102*–103
Nuts and seeds
    about: natural peanut butter, 116
    Almond-Crusted Tilapia, 104
    Banana-Peanut Butter Smoothie, 14
    Flourless Chocolate Hazelnut Cake, *112*, 120
    Hazelnut & Fruit Granola, 16
    Morning Glory Muffins, *24*–25
    Peanut Butter Cookies, 116
    Peanut Sauce, 72–*73*
    Warm Quinoa Salad with Toasted Almonds, 40–*41*

Oatmeal-Chocolate Chip Cookies, 115
Oats, in Hazelnut & Fruit Granola, 16

Pad Thai, 64
Pancakes, buckwheat, 22
Pasta
    Caramelized Chili Shrimp Stir-Fry, 71
    Home-Style Pad Thai, 64
    Mixed Vegetable Minestrone, 47
    Spaghetti Squash "Pasta" Puttanesca, *74*–75
    Vietnamese Rice Noodle Soup, 55
Peanuts. *See* Nuts and seeds
Peppers, in Ratatouille on the Grill, 93
Peppers, in Sausage-Pepper Kabobs, *84*–85
Pineapple, grilled, jerk pork chops with, *76*, 83
Pizza, homemade, 108–*109*
Polenta & Spinach Gratin, 110
Pomegranate-Berry Smoothie, 14–*15*
Pork
    about: bacon and gluten, 44
    Brazilian-Style Pork Chops, 62
    Chilled Corn & Bacon Soup, 44–*45*
    Jerk Pork Chops with Grilled Pineapple, *76*, 83
    Mushroom-Glazed Pork Chops, 100–*101*
    New Orleans Pork & Charred Beans, *102*–103
    Pork Posole, 54
    Sausage-Pepper Kabobs, *84*–85
    Stuffed Acorn Squash, 111
Potatoes
    Chicken with Smashed Potatoes, Potpie Style, 63
    Potato-Crusted Quiche, 20–*21*
    Roasted Cod with Potatoes & Kale, 105
Poultry
    Chicken & Apple Meat Loaves, *94*, 99
    Chicken Tikka Masala, 58–*59*
    Chicken with Smashed Potatoes, Potpie Style, 63
    Coffee-Spiced Chicken with Fruit-Basil Salsa, 80–*81*
    Coq au Riesling, *42*, 52
    Curried Chicken Pitas, 30–*31*
    Espresso-Balsamic Roasted Chicken, *96*–97

Herbed Skillet Chicken, 98
Jerk Turkey Burgers, 82
Mango Chicken Lettuce Cups, 34–*35*
Sweet & Tangy Barbecued Chicken, 78–*79*
Szechuan Chicken Pasta with Peanut Sauce, 72–*73*
Vietnamese Rice Noodle Soup, 55
Pumpkin Crème Caramel, *118*–119

Quinoa, about, 11
Quinoa salad, warm, 40–*41*

Rice and wild rice
    about: types of rice, 11; wild rice, 11
    Chicken & Mushrooms with Brown Rice, *60*–61
    Rice & Bean Burgers, 28
    Spring Vegetable Risotto with Shrimp, *56*, 70
    Stuffed Acorn Squash, 111
    Tangerine Beef Stir-Fry, 65
    Vietnamese Rice Noodle Soup, 55
Roasted Cod with Potatoes & Kale, 105

Salads
    about: overview of recipes, 27
    Edamame Salad, 90–*91*
    Korean Steak in Lettuce Cups, 86–*87*
    Lentil Salad with Shrimp, Apples & Mint, *38*–39
    Mango Chicken Lettuce Cups, 34–*35*
    Salad Niçoise, *26*, 36
    Six-Bean Salad with Tomato Vinaigrette, 37
    Warm Quinoa Salad with Toasted Almonds, 40–*41*
Sandwiches and wraps
    about: bread to use, 27; overview of recipes, 27
    Curried Chicken Pitas, 30–*31*
    Homemade Sandwich Bread, 29
    Jerk Turkey Burgers, 82
    Korean Steak in Lettuce Cups, 86–*87*
    Mango Chicken Lettuce Cups, 34–*35*
    Open-Faced Smoked Salmon Sandwiches, *32*–33
    Rice & Bean Burgers, 28
Sauces
    Fruit-Basil Salsa, 80–*81*
    Green Sauce, 66
    Peanut Sauce, 72–*73*
    Tomato Vinaigrette, 37
Sausage-Pepper Kabobs, *84*–85
Smoothies, 14
Sorghum flour, in All-Purpose Flour Blend, 114
Soups & stews, 43–55
    about: overview of recipes, 43
    Chilled Corn & Bacon Soup, 44–*45*
    Coq au Riesling, *42*, 52
    Fish Stew, *48*–49
    Healthy Makeover Beef Burgundy, 50–*51*
    Mixed Vegetable Minestrone, 47
    Pork Posole, 54
    Tomato Soup with Tofu-Parmesan Croutons, 46
    Valentine's Day Red Chili, 53
    Vietnamese Rice Noodle Soup, 55
Spinach, in Polenta & Spinach Gratin, 110
Spring Vegetable Risotto with Shrimp, *56*, 70

Squash
    Mexican Veggie Stacks, 92
    Ratatouille on the Grill, 93
    Spaghetti Squash "Pasta" Puttanesca, *74*–75
    Stuffed Acorn Squash, 111
Steak. *See* Beef
Stovetop suppers, 57–75
    about: overview of recipes, 57
    Brazilian-Style Pork Chops, 62
    Caramelized Chili Shrimp Stir-Fry, 71
    Chicken and Mushrooms with Brown Rice, *60*–61
    Chicken Tikka Masala, 58–*59*
    Chicken with Smashed Potatoes, Potpie Style, 63
    Home-Style Pad Thai, 64
    Spaghetti Squash "Pasta" Puttanesca, *74*–75
    Spring Vegetable Risotto with Shrimp, *56*, 70
    Steak & Tomato Sauté, *68*–69
    Steaks with Green Sauce, 66–*67*
    Szechuan Chicken Pasta with Peanut Sauce, 72–*73*
    Tangerine Beef Stir-Fry, 65
Stuffed Acorn Squash, 111
Sweet & Tangy Barbecued Chicken, 78–*79*
Sweets, 113–123. *See also* Chocolate
    about: overview of recipes, 113
    All-Purpose Flour Blend, 114
    Banana-Berry Parfaits, 122–*123*
    Flourless Chocolate Hazelnut Cake, *112*
    Lemon Meringue Drops, 117
    Peanut Butter Cookies, 116
    Pumpkin Crème Caramel, *118*–119
    Szechuan Chicken Pasta with Peanut Sauce, 72–*73*

Teff, about, 11
30-minutes-or-less Recipes icon, 7
Tofu
    Home-Style Pad Thai, 64
    Tofu-Parmesan Croutons, 46
Tomatoes
    Crustless Tomato-Ricotta Pie, *12*, 17
    Mexican Veggie Stacks, 92
    Ratatouille on the Grill, 93
    Steak & Tomato Sauté, *68*–69
    Tomato Soup with Tofu-Parmesan Croutons, 46
    Tomato Vinaigrette, 37
    Valentine's Day Red Chili, 53
Turkey. *See* Poultry

Valentine's Day Red Chili, 53
Vegetables. *See also specific vegetables*
    Mexican Veggie Stacks, 92
    Ratatouille on the Grill, 93
    soups with. *See* Soups and stews
Vietnamese Rice Noodle Soup, 55

Xanthan gum, about, 23

Yogurt
    about: flavored/flavoring, 14
    Banana-Berry Parfaits, 122–*123*
    Pomegranate-Berry Smoothie, 14–*15*

Photography Credits

Metric Conversion Charts

The recipes that appear in this cookbook use the standard United States method for measuring liquid and dry or solid ingredients (teaspoons, tablespoons, and cups). The information on this chart is provided to help cooks outside the U.S. successfully use these recipes. All equivalents are approximate.

METRIC EQUIVALENTS FOR DIFFERENT TYPES OF INGREDIENTS

STANDARD CUP (e.g. flour)	FINE POWDER (e.g. rice)	GRAIN (e.g. sugar)	GRANULAR (e.g. butter)	LIQUID SOLIDS (e.g. milk)	LIQUID
3/4	105 g	113 g	143 g	150 g	180 ml
2/3	93 g	100 g	125 g	133 g	160 ml
1/2	70 g	75 g	95 g	100 g	120 ml
1/3	47 g	50 g	63 g	67 g	80 ml
1/4	35 g	38 g	48 g	50 g	60 ml
1/8	18 g	19 g	24 g	25 g	30 ml

USEFUL EQUIVALENTS FOR LIQUID INGREDIENTS BY VOLUME

1/4 tsp	=					1 ml
1/2 tsp	=					2 ml
1 tsp	=					5 ml
3 tsp	=	1 tbls	=	1/2 fl oz	=	15 ml
		2 tbls	=	1/8 cup	=	1 fl oz	=	30 ml
		4 tbls	=	1/4 cup	=	2 fl oz	=	60 ml
		5 1/8 tbls	=	1/3 cup	=	3 fl oz	=	80 ml
		8 tbls	=	1/2 cup	=	4 fl oz	=	120 ml
		10 2/8 tbls	=	2/3 cup	=	5 fl oz	=	160 ml
		12 tbls	=	3/4 cup	=	6 fl oz	=	180 ml
		16 tbls	=	1 cup	=	8 fl oz	=	240 ml
		1 pt	=	2 cups	=	16 fl oz	=	480 ml
		1 qt	=	4 cups	=	32 fl oz	=	960 ml
						33 fl oz	=	1000 ml = 1 L

USEFUL EQUIVALENTS FOR DRY INGREDIENTS BY WEIGHT

(To convert ounces to grams, multiply the number of ounces by 30.)

1 oz	=	1/16 lb	=	30 g
4 oz	=	1/4 lb	=	120 g
8 oz	=	1/2 lb	=	240 g
12 oz	=	3/4 lb	=	360 g
16 oz	=	1 lb	=	480 g

USEFUL EQUIVALENTS FOR COOKING/OVEN TEMPERATURES

	Fahrenheit	Celsius	Gas Mark
Freeze Water	32° F	0° C	
Room Temperature	68° F	20° C	
Boil Water	212° F	100° C	
Bake	325° F	160° C	3
	350° F	180° C	4
	375° F	190° C	5
	400° F	200° C	6
	425° F	220° C	7
	450° F	230° C	8
Broil			Grill

USEFUL EQUIVALENTS LENGTH

(To convert inches to centimeters, multiply the number of inches by 2.5.)

1 in	=					2.5 cm		
6 in	=	1/2 ft	=			15 cm		
12 in	=	1 ft	=			30 cm		
36 in	=	3 ft	=	1 yd	=	90 cm		
40 in	=					100 cm	=	1 m

THE GOOD HOUSEKEEPING
TRIPLE-TEST PROMISE

At *Good Housekeeping*, we want to make sure that every recipe we print works in any oven, with any brand of ingredient, no matter what. That's why, in our test kitchens at the **Good Housekeeping Research Institute**, we go all out: We test each recipe at least three times—and, often, several more times after that.

When a recipe is first developed, one member of our team prepares the dish, and we judge it on these criteria: It must be **delicious**, **family-friendly**, **healthy**, and **easy to make**.

1 The recipe is then tested several more times to fine-tune the flavor and ease of preparation, always by the same team member, using the same equipment.

2 Next, another team member follows the recipe as written, **varying the brands of ingredients** and **kinds of equipment**. Even the types of stoves we use are changed.

3 A third team member repeats the whole process **using yet another set of equipment** and **alternative ingredients**. By the time the recipes appear on these pages, they are guaranteed to work in any kitchen, including yours. **We promise**.